D0902132

JEWISH PARENTING

JEWISH PARENTING

Rabbinic Insights

Judith Z. Abrams
Steven A. Abrams

JASON ARONSON, INC.
Northvale, New Jersey
London

The authors gratefully acknowledge permission to quote from the following sources:
From *The Midrash on Proverbs*, translated from the Hebrew with an introduction and annotations by Burton L. Visotzky. Copyright © 1992 by Yale University Press. Used by permission of the publisher, Yale University Press.
From *The Tosefta*, edited and translated from the Hebrew by Jacob Neusner. Copyright © 1977, 1979, 1981, 1986 by Jacob Neusner. Used by permission of KTAV Publishing House.
From "Report of the Task Force on Circumcision," by the American Academy of Pediatrics Task Force on Circumcision, *Pediatrics*, vol. 84, pp. 388–391. Copyright © 1989 by the American Academy of Pediatrics. Used by permission of *Pediatrics*.
From "The Pediatrician and Corporal Punishment," by M. A. Wessel, *Pediatrics*, vol. 66, pp. 639–640. Copyright © 1980 by the American Academy of Pediatrics. Used by permission of *Pediatrics*.

This book was set in 12 pt. Korinna by Alpha Graphics of Pittsfield, New Hampshire, and printed by Haddon Craftsmen in Scranton, Pennsylvania.

Library of Congress Cataloging-in-Publication Data

Abrams, Judith Z.
    Jewish parenting : rabbinic insights / Judith Z.
Abrams, Steven A. Abrams.
        p.   cm
    Includes bibliographical references and index.
    ISBN 1-56821-175-9
    1. Child rearing—Religious aspects—Judaism.   2. Education in rabbinical literature.   3. Rabbinical literature—History and criticism.   I. Abrams, Steven A.   II. Title.
HQ769.3.A27   1994
296.7'4—dc20   94-6114

Manufactured in the United States of America. Jason Aronson Inc. offers books and cassettes. For information and catalog write to Jason Aronson Inc., 230 Livingston Street, Northvale, New Jersey 07647.

To our children,
Michael, Ruth, and Hannah

Contents

PART III: SEPARATION

9 Adolescence and Jewish Parenting   223

Preface
and Acknowledgments

The Aim of This Book

The bedrock of Judaism is expressed in the Shema: God is one. There is no aspect of our world and experience of which we can say, "God is not a part of this." Our physical selves, our emotions, our intellects, our spirits, are all integrated in Judaism.

Our experience as parents probably brings home this truth more clearly than any other facet of our lives. We are charged with the physical, emotional, intellectual, and spiritual well-being and development of our children. To ignore one of these realms is to be incomplete, and perhaps harmful, as parents.

Let us be clear from the start: this is not strictly a historical outline of the way children were raised in the rabbinic era (70–500 C.E.). Nor is it a medical text or a guide to Jewish law regarding child care. Likewise, it is not merely a personal account of our own experiences. Rather, it is a combination of historical, medical, Jewish, and personal insights into raising children. By drawing on these varied sources, we hope to reflect the complexity of parenting and draw on as many sources of information as possible to shed light on this most important topic in our lives. And by presenting texts from rabbinic literature itself, we hope to open the world of that literature to parents who are searching for the wisdom of our Sages as they strive to raise healthy, happy, Jewish children, as well as those who want to explore the history of Jewish medicine.

Some Notes on Style and Translations

A few words should be said about the style of this book. Indented passages are selections from the *Tanach* (the Jewish Bible), rabbinic literature, and medical sources. Passages in italics relate our own personal experiences as parents, physician, or rabbi. Initials, SAA for Steven, and JZA for Judith, indicate the source of the comment. Bavli passages are cited according to their traditional folio numbers from the Babylonian Talmud and passages from the Yerushalmi are cited according to the Venice Edition. The word *Mishnah* with a capital *M* indicates the entire work: all six tractates. The word *mishnah* with a lowercase *m* indicates a passage from that work.

The translations of rabbinic literature used in this book are adapted from Jacob Neusner's translations of Tosefta and the Yerushalmi, the Soncino translation of *Midrash Rabbah*, Vizotsky's translation of Midrash on Proverbs, and the Soncino translation of the Babylonian Talmud edited by Maurice Simon. Although we have used gender-inclusive language in our text, the translations reflect that the language used to describe God in rabbinic literature is most often in the male gender. Instead of using *he/she* or *him/her*, we have used male and female pronouns in alternating chapters, unless one gender is clearly indicated by the material at hand (e.g., when discussing circumcision).

Acknowledgments

We are grateful to God for the opportunity to write this book together. The following individuals have helped us in this process. Max Mintz, M.D., pediatrician and *mohel*, read the manuscript most carefully and made many excellent suggestions. Rabbi Joseph Radinsky, Tomas Silber, M.D., Buford Nichols, M.D., Judy Hopkinson, Ph.D., Janice Fagen, M.S.W., and David Kraemer, Ph.D., also read the manuscript and made many valuable comments. We appreciate the time and effort they took. Professor Jonathan Sarna provided us with historical information on Jewish demographics. The librarians of the Baylor College of Medicine, Hebrew Union College–Jewish Institute of Religion in Cincinnati, and Congregation Beth Yeshurun in Houston were also most helpful in providing us with information. We are deeply grateful to our publisher, Jason Aronson, Inc., especially Arthur Kurzweil, Marion Cino, and Jean Pease, for helping us bring this book to fruition. Finally, we are most indebted to our children, Michael, Ruth, and Hannah, for inspiring us to write this work . . . and for allowing us to complete it!

I

Introductions

1

Introduction to Rabbinic Literature

Rabbinic Literature and the Modern Parent

When we think of rabbinic literature and the people who study it, we may imagine old men poring over huge volumes written in Hebrew, tracing obscure points of Jewish law through stacks of books. We don't tend to think of parents with children, racing from the grocery store to school, to work, to music lessons, to dentist appointments, studying rabbinic literature. First of all, they don't have the luxury of sufficient time to study for hours each day (not to mention the fact that doing it in Hebrew might present a bit of a problem). And second, rabbinic literature, at first glance, doesn't seem terribly "user friendly." Yet these books have much to teach modern families and are not as inaccessible as they might seem. The study of rabbinic literature might best be described as an acquired taste, and like any acquired taste, it's better to nibble than to gorge oneself. In this book, we attempt to provide small bits, particularly those that can provide insights on raising healthy and happy children and more fully enjoying parenting.

A common misconception about Talmud and rabbinic literature is that you have to know Hebrew, be a rabbi, or be a devout Jew to even look at it. Nothing could be further from the truth. Rabbinic literature is often described as a sea, so just jump in and swim around until you figure out what works best and feels right to you. It belongs to every Jew and every person interested in Judaism. [JZA]

The Short Course

Readers who are interested in the history of rabbinic literature and want to know about the literary characteristics of its component documents and their relationship to each other should consult the rest of this chapter. For those who are not really interested in the background of rabbinic literature, here is a short description. Rabbinic literature records the thoughts and lives of sages (rabbis) who lived and taught between 70 and 500 c.e. in the Land of Israel and in Babylonia. These teachings explain the Torah's rulings and form the basis for Jewish practice and thought to this day.

The Long Course: The Five Main Components of Rabbinic Literature

Rabbinic literature is made up of five major kinds of works. Because we draw on all five sources of material in this

ese Five Works as "People"

w do these five kinds of rabbinic literature differ from
:h other? In general, the Mishnah, which was compiled
t, contains an outline of how the law given in the writ-
Torah is to be followed. Its contents are more theo-
cal than practical. Practical details are provided by the
sefta, the Yerushalmi, and the Bavli. The Midrash col-
tions are unique in that they are made up principally
stories, sermons, or passages that expound biblical
ses rather than focusing primarily on Jewish law and
ctice.

One way to understand the interrelationship of these
binic writings is to think about them as different per-
ality types. The Mishnah is like a dreamer who's al-
ys imagining how things should be rather than think-
about how they are. This sort of person constantly
ncocts beautiful schemes to organize her life. The only
blem is that these dreams don't necessarily corre-
ond with reality.

Tosefta is like the Mishnah's more practical friend.
en the Mishnah goes off on an idealistic tangent,
sefta says, "Wait a minute. I don't think that's going to
rk the way you think it's going to. And what if condi-
ns change? And have you thought of all the conse-
ences?"

The Yerushalmi is like Tosefta, only more so. The
rushalmi listens to the Mishnah and Tosefta and then
kes over the conversation, citing statistics and infor-
ation from a vast library of knowledge. The Yerushalmi
ay take a long time to come to a decision, but usually
will eventually tell you that "Yes, the Mishnah's plan
ll work" or "No, the Mishnah's plan won't work, but

volume, a brief introduction to each of these
order. The five main works are (1) the Mishn
Tosefta, (3) the Talmud of the Land of Israe
shalmi), (4) the Midrash collections, and (5) t
of Babylonia (the Bavli). Those parts of the Ta
are commentary on the Mishnah are called Ge
commonly used term *Talmud* refers to the M
Gemara combined.

Rabbinic literature is frequently called the (
Tradition has it that Moses received the laws ai
contained in the Oral Torah from God on Mou
the same time he was given the Written Tora
five books of the Bible). This Oral Torah was pa
through the generations, "from Moses to Josh
to the elders; the elders to the prophets" (*M.*
1:1). Some scholars believe that the teachings
Torah developed during a much later peric
less of the time of its genesis, the Oral Tor
Sages' method of making the Written Toral
ful to the people of their day. The following tal
rizes important historical information about t
works of rabbinic literature and the abbreviat
use to identify these texts along with the nar
vidual tractates, that is, individual books (
Torah.

	Date Finished	Place Finished	Abb
Mishnah	200 C.E.	The Land of Israel	*M.*+
Tosefta	220–230 C.E.	The Land of Israel	*T.* +
Yerushalmi	400 C.E.	The Land of Israel	*Y.* +
Midrash	400–500 C.E.	The Land of Israel	full
Bavli	427–560 C.E.	Babylonia	*B.* +

Tosefta's might" or "Neither the Mishnah nor the Tosefta has it right. However, I have an answer that I think *will* work."

The Midrash collections, which comment on different books of the Bible rather than on the Mishnah, as does the rest of rabbinic literature, are loners. They're loosely connected to the Mishnah, Tosefta, Yerushalmi, and Bavli, but they really go their own way. They're like that one member of a circle of friends who is included, but not terribly attached. And are they into telling stories! The difference between the Mishnah and the Midrash collections is that the Mishnah wants to pretend that her dreams are going to shape reality. The Midrash collections want to tell stories and find meaning and enjoyment in life without necessarily legislating that vision. It's sort of like the difference between an idealistic politician (the Mishnah) and a political commentator (the Midrash collections): one is into prescribing solutions, the other into talking about problems and brainstorming ideas.

Finally, the Bavli is like the Yerushalmi . . . and not like the Yerushalmi. Like the Yerushalmi, the Bavli listens to the Mishnah and Tosefta and then takes over the conversation. However, unlike the Yerushalmi, the Bavli isn't so "bottom line" oriented. The Bavli is often more interested in exploring options than in determining the one right solution to a problem. Also, the Bavli loves to tell stories; almost as much as the Midrash collections do. Finally, the Bavli is a bit more talkative than the Yerushalmi—who is already quite talkative.

If you ever gathered these five "people" in a room, Mishnah would start the conversation. Next, Tosefta would get in a few comments. Then the conversation would be taken over by the Yerushalmi and the Bavli. The Midrash collections would be over in a corner studying Torah, listening to the conversation, and occasionally contributing to it. Let us eavesdrop on such a conversation now.

The Five Works and the Nursing Mother

We will explore the different characteristics of the five kinds of rabbinic literature by contrasting their approaches to a single topic that touches on pediatrics: a mother's obligation to nurse her child. The *mishnah* we will study outlines a wife's obligations to her husband and the ways she may fulfill them:

> These are the tasks that a wife does for her husband: she grinds corn, and bakes and does washing, cooks and nurses her child, makes his bed [for him], and works in wool. If she brought him one servant woman, she need not grind nor bake nor wash; if two, she does not have to cook, nor nurse her child; if three, she is not required to make his bed [for him], nor work in wool; if four, she may sit on a raised seat. (*M. Ketubot* 5:5)

These are rather idealized rules. If a woman has no servants, she must perform the household duties outlined above. Note that she makes an economic contribution to her household by working in wool. In the Mishnah's idealized world, which was based, in part, on a vision of Israel living in villages in the Land of Israel with a functioning Temple, one archetypal occupation was that of shepherd, so the archetypal wife was to help process the wool of the flock. If she has servants to help her, she may delegate her work to them. What is important for our purposes is that the woman is obligated to nurse her child, or provide for nursing, as one of her basic wifely duties.

Tosefta brings a new dimension to the material in the Mishnah, adding some "real-world" factors to the Mishnah's idealized view. In the Mishnah, rules are simply expressed as universal principles. In Tosefta, there is a bit more concern with the actual application of these rules. For example, Tosefta addresses the question, "What if the woman doesn't want to nurse her child?"

> If her son recognized her [as his mother], they give her a wage, and she nurses him, because of the danger [to the child's life]. (*T. Ketubot* 5:5)

Tosefta describes what should be done if the child wants to nurse from his mother but she does not wish to nurse him. (In Tosefta, this specific example concerns a divorced woman and the way nursing interferes with her plans to remarry.) In such a case, her ex-husband pays her a wage to nurse the child and she is then compelled to nurse him herself because, there being no alternative nutrition for the child, the Sages feared the child would die if not provided with the sustenance that he preferred. This is just one of Tosefta's many comments on this mishnah. Still, we see how much more detailed it is. It is the difference between an ideal vision of the world and a nuts-and-bolts operational interpretation of that vision.

Much of the Gemara (i.e., the commentary on the Mishnah in the Talmuds) is based on Tosefta. However, the Gemara in both the Yerushalmi and the Bavli is even more detailed than Tosefta in its explanation of the Mishnah. Here, as is often the case, the Gemara begins by quoting the relevant passage from Tosefta, then adding to it.

> She nurses her child (*M. Ketubot* 5:5). . . . If her son recognized her [as his mother], they give her a wage, and

she nurses him, because of the danger [to the child's life].
(*T. Ketubot* 5:5). . . . Under what circumstances [can
she refuse to nurse]? In a case in which the infant does
not recognize the mother. But if he recognizes her, they
force her [to nurse him] and pay her a wage to nurse her
child.

And how old would he be so as to recognize her? Rabbi
Jeremiah in the name of Rav: "Three months." Now [when
he made that statement], Rabbi Zeira cast his gaze at him.
He said to him, "Why are you staring at me? Shall I tell
you what Samuel said? For Samuel said, 'Three days.'"

Samuel is consistent with opinions expressed elsewhere. Samuel said, "I recognized the midwife who delivered me [right after I was born]." Rabbi Joshua ben Levi
said, "I recognized the *mohel* who performed the circumcision on me." Rabbi Yohanan said, "I recognized the
women who kept my mother company [during labor]."
(*Y. Ketubot* 5:6, 30a)

The Sages wonder how long it takes for a child to recognize its mother and be willing to nurse only from her. An
opinion is voiced that this takes three months, but Rabbi
Zeira is apparently skeptical that a child could recognize
its mother as early as three months, to which Rabbi Jeremiah replies that a child can recognize its mother as early
as the third day of life. This statement is then further supported by statements of three other Sages who were able
to recognize individuals at quite young ages. (As we will
see in subsequent chapters, some recent studies have
suggested that a child learns to recognize its mother's
voice and smell in the first week of life.) However, the
suggestions that an infant might remember the midwife
or *mohel* are highly unlikely and even humorous.

The Gemara of the Babylonian Talmud, the Bavli, is

even more elaborate. In general, as we pointed out earlier, we will find this to be the case when we contrast the Yerushalmi and the Bavli. To see the difference in the Bavli's approach, let's examine what it has to say with regard to the mishnah we've been studying. We'll see the trends we found in the Yerushalmi amplified in the Bavli:

> Nursing her child (*M. Ketubot* 5:5). . . . If [the child] knows her (*T. Ketubot* 5:5, 60a) [up to] what age [can she refuse to nurse]? Rava in the name of Rav Jeremiah bar Abba who had it from Rav said: Three months. Samuel, however, said: Thirty days, while Rabbi Isaac stated in the name of Rabbi Yohanan: Fifty days. Rav Shimi bar Abaye stated: Jewish law is in agreement with the statement of Rabbi Isaac which was made in the name of Rabbi Yohanan.
>
> One can well understand [the respective views of] Rav and Rabbi Yohanan since they are guided by the child's keenness of perception. According to Samuel, however, is such [precocity] at all possible?—When Rami bar Ezekiel came [from the Land of Israel to Babylonia] he said, "Pay no regard to those rules which my brother Judah laid down in the name of Samuel; for thus said Samuel: As soon as [the child] knows her." (*B. Ketubot* 59b–60a)

In commenting on the Mishnah's edict that a woman must nurse her child, the Bavli cites Tosefta's ruling that if the child knows the mother, she is compelled to nurse him because, if she did not, it would constitute a danger to the child. Then we find three conflicting traditions as to when a child recognizes its mother: at 90 days, at 30 days, and at 50 days. Jewish law is then determined to be the compromise position of 50 days.

Further comment is made on this difference of opinion among the Sages. The two differing views of Rav (90
days) and Rabbi Yohanan (50 days) can be explained as
based on the difference between children with less keen
and more keen perception, respectively. Samuel's view
is apparently deemed completely unrealistic. We then
learn that an authority who was familiar with Samuel's
teachings dismisses the version we have here and attributes to him a teaching consistent with Tosefta's: no
matter what the age the child is when he recognizes his
mother, she is thereafter obligated to nurse him. (There
is obviously some confusion about Samuel's teachings
on this subject: in the Yerushalmi we learned that he believed an infant first recognized its mother at 3 days, and
in the Bavli his opinion is quoted as being either 30 days
or simply when the child knows its mother.) Regardless
of when they thought a child recognized its mother, Samuel and the other Sages were apparently quite interested
in a child's development and his relationship with his
mother and considered that relationship to be very important for the child's health.

The Midrash collections are less concerned with practical, legal problems than with moral lessons and parables.
They differ from the other kinds of rabbinic literature in
that Midrash is intended for both scholars and laypersons,
while the Mishnah, Tosefta, and Talmuds were intended
primarily for scholarly audiences. The contrast is something like the difference between popular histories of how
the Constitution developed, which explain the meaning
of the Constitution for the average reader, and actual
books of constitutional law codes. The emphasis of one
sort of book is on meaning; the emphasis of the other is
on detail and definition. Midrash also differs from other

types of rabbinic literature in that it is organized according to the order of the Torah and other biblical books rather than the order of the Mishnah.

The issue of weaning and nursing is touched upon in the Midrash collections. For example, we have this explication of Genesis 21:8:

> "And the child [Isaac] grew (*vayigdal*), and was weaned" (Genesis 21:8). R. Hoshaya the Elder said: He was weaned from his evil inclination. Sages said: He was weaned from his mother's milk. (*Genesis Rabbah* 53:10)

Isaac's weaning, indeed the weaning of any child in due course in the ancient world, was a moment for great celebration since so many children died before reaching this stage of life. Therefore, it seems natural that Abraham would rejoice that his son Isaac had survived to this age and that this phase of his life was past.

The Sages' interest is piqued by the way this verse is phrased. The Sages thought that a child was grown (*vayigdal*) at the age of 13. So some Sages think this verse says, "Isaac reached 13 years of age and was weaned." Well, if Isaac was 13 years old, he was obviously not being weaned from his mother's milk. So what could he have been weaned from? At thirteen, the Sages believed that one could begin to dominate one's urge to do evil (the *yetser hara*), and so they suggest that Isaac was weaned from his evil inclination. However, other Sages state that the verse should be understood in its simple meaning: Isaac was weaned from his mother's milk. This short passage exemplifies one of the Midrash collections' most endearing qualities: their willingness to interpret the Torah with great imagination, and their willingness to admit that there is a straightforward way of interpreting it, too. Because both sorts of interpretations are included, we are encouraged to look at the Torah with all our sharpness of mind; to appreciate Torah in both fanciful and serious ways, since Torah has many levels of meaning.

Torah is said to speak in seventy tongues. That is, we can understand it in many ways. From it we can derive the idealistic vision of a Jewish world found in the Mishnah and the more detailed outlines of how to live a Jewish life found in the Tosefta, Yerushalmi, and Bavli. We can also find there the imaginative language of the Midrash collections. Another language that the Torah speaks in, the language of Jewish law, is a language we will not explore in this volume. Although most of the precedents for Jewish law are contained in the Mishnah and Talmuds, the works that codified Jewish law, such as Maimonides' *Mishneh Torah* or Karo's *Shulhan Aruch*, were written long after the period we are considering here and are a different kind of literature altogether. Hence, we will not be examining them in this volume.

We might note here that some Jews consider the legal pronouncements in rabbinic literature as binding on their lives, while some do not. Sometimes it is easier to understand what rabbinic literature is saying if you aren't concerned with having to follow what it says, just as it is sometimes easier to clearly hear what your co-worker is saying rather than what your boss is saying. As we will see, some of the teachings, particularly the medical guidelines, contained in rabbinic literature cannot be directly applied today in the context of modern medical care. We can just appreciate this material for giving us a picture of life as it was conducted centuries ago. [SAA, JZA]

Options and Guidance for Modern Parents

For a parent, one of the most comforting features of rabbinic literature is one of its most constant features, as well: argumentation. Argumentation is the purposeful presentation of differing points of view. We already saw the tendency toward argumentation in our Yerushalmi and Bavli passage, above: several different definitions of when a child recognizes his mother are mentioned as possibly valid. In other words, there is seldom only one right answer to problems, and the Sages recognized that fact. So they offered many different possible answers that all have a degree of validity, since they are all included in rabbinic literature. This means that the tradition preserves alternative answers for parents searching for guidance, and in this volume we hope to present those alternatives.

One other feature of these works must be made clear before we begin. Much of rabbinic literature is legal in nature. Therefore, it describes minimum standards of behavior that must be upheld. However, the minimum requirements of law and what is optimal or ideal are often quite different from each other, particularly with regard to the parent–child relationship. For example, you can't legislate that a child should frequently be taken to the library; you can only encourage it. The Sages legislated the minimum requirements of parenting but hoped parents would go beyond this minimum in caring for their children. Many of these wishes are expressed, not as laws, but as actions that God will reward.

Things haven't changed much in the past 1,500 years. As a rabbi serving a medium-sized congregation in Missouri City, Texas (a suburb of Houston), I, like the

*Sages of the Talmud, cannot issue edicts and force
people to practice Judaism the way I think they
should. All I, or any rabbi, for that matter, can do is
offer attractive Jewish options that can persuade
people to participate in Jewish life more fully.* [JZA]

A Bridge to Our Past

Rabbinic literature provides us with a bridge to our past.
It is connected to our lives today because so many of its
insights are still valid in terms of living a Jewish life and
being good parents. It also connects us to ideas that be-
long in the past: medical concepts that we no longer
believe are valid. If we are to understand the Sages' guidelines for child rearing, we must understand the world in
which they lived and the ideas they held about the body
that were strongly influenced by Greek, Roman, and Babylonian cultures. It is to this history of medicine that we now
turn our attention.

2

The History of Pediatrics and Rabbinic Medicine

To understand the Sages' writings about pediatrics, we must place these works in their historical context. We must imagine ourselves in a world in which parents could have ten children, only two or three of whom would live to adulthood. We must imagine a world where disease is ever-present and we are all but powerless to affect its course. We must imagine a world in which Jews are considered strange because they raise all of their children, disabled or not, instead of practicing infanticide, as the Greeks and Romans did. When we understand this context, some of the Sages' teachings will become more understandable to us.

The Short Course

As with the history of rabbinic literature, the history of medicine as it relates to the era of the Sages can be described briefly or in more detail. Some of this detail is considered in the rest of this chapter. For those who consider a chapter about the history of medicine to be as exciting as a lecture on the life cycle of the salamander, feel free to omit this and head on to the next chapter. In that case, one can summarize the history of medicine by noting that the era of the Sages was one in which the basics of physiology were unknown, antibiotics were nonexistent, and life spans were relatively short. In particular, infant mortality was high, as was maternal mortality from childbirth.

The Long Course:
Infanticide and Infant Mortality

Jews differed from the ancient Greeks and Romans with regard to infanticide. Jews (and Egyptians and Germans) raised all their children and did not "expose them," as the practice of infanticide was called. The Greeks and Romans found this odd, for they frequently practiced infanticide, although it was less common among the Romans until the waning days of the empire. Numerous edicts against infanticide were issued by various Roman emperors between 300 and 500 C.E., and early Christian leaders spoke out against it.[1] Infanticide was also widespread among Eastern cultures throughout ancient and medieval history.

Even if allowed to survive past birth, many children died during the first years of life. This problem has only recently diminished. As late as the nineteenth century, even in the United States and Europe, infant mortality was a major concern. For example, in 1815 in England, approximately 25 percent of children died before their second birthday,

50 percent before their fifth birthday.[2] These rates did not begin to decline significantly until around 1870 with the introduction of improved sanitation and, in the early twentieth century, with the rise of social activism on behalf of children. A gradual decrease to less than 10 percent infant mortality did not occur until well after the beginning of the twentieth century. The rate has gradually declined to current levels of approximately 1 percent mortality in the first year of life in Western countries.[3]

Infant Mortality and the Jewish People

We do not have accurate infant mortality statistics for the Sages' era. However, we do have them for much more recent years. Naturally, great caution should be used when drawing conclusions from two eras so widely separated in time. Nonetheless, even these recent statistics can shed light on this issue.

In the early part of the twentieth century in the United States, efforts were made to improve the poor social conditions associated with high infant mortality rates. Interestingly, several authors of that era commented on the lower infant mortality rates in Jewish communities as compared to the general population. In 1906 one medical writer noted: "Perhaps no part of the population of our great cities [in the United States] suffer so much upon the whole from overcrowding and bad housing as the poorest class of Jews, yet the mortality of infants among them is much less than among the poor of other nationalities."[4] In 1915 another writer made the explicit connection between the value Jews place on their children and the good health of those children: "Infant mortality in the crowded Jewish quarters of towns is always low, in spite of overcrowding, defective housing and poverty, because the Jewish people set a great deal of store by home life and affection for children is strong among them."[5]

Yet another study, in which infant mortality rates among American Jews were compared with those rates among the general population from 1885 to 1890, corroborates these observations. During that period, infant mortality was approximately 80 per 1,000 for Jews versus 165 per 1,000 for the general population. In addition, life expectancy for Jews was approximately 13 years longer (56 vs. 43 years, compared to 70 to 80 years today). When we consider our ancient sources, we must bear in mind the prevalence of death in that era, particularly among children.

The State of the Sages' Medical Knowledge

While many of the Sages' medical beliefs and teachings about raising children correspond to modern medicine and child-rearing techniques, some of them do not. We cannot reasonably compare the Sages' knowledge of medicine with our own. The most fundamental concepts of physiology and medicine, including, for example, the process of conception, the functioning of the circulatory system, and the nature of microorganisms, were unknown in ancient days. Rather, the ancients ascribed medical conditions to what they could see and, at times, to what we might currently consider magical beliefs. Nonetheless, lacking significant medical instrumentation and pharmaceuticals, the ancients were precise observers.

To demonstrate the difference between medicine then and now, for example, we need look no further than a very long segment of the Babylonian Talmud, in tractate *Gittin* (*B. Gittin* 68b–70b), which outlines many medical beliefs of the Sages. We learn there that

> [f]or night blindness he should take a string made of white hair and with it tie one of his own legs to the leg of a dog, and children should rattle potsherds behind him saying "old dog, stupid cock." (*B. Gittin* 69a)

This passage reflects the ancient belief in transference of medical ills. In this case, it was believed that the night blindness could be transferred to the dog. Rabbinic literature contains other, similar practices. For example, the Sages believed in demons who could harm individuals and cause illnesses.

It is not our purpose to specify the obvious differences between medical practice in ancient days and modern medical care or even to attempt to determine the exact nature of the various diseases and treatments described in the Bible and rabbinic literature. Rather, it is our intent to show how the Sages thought about the body and its diseases and to examine the many social and moral lessons they drew from medicine.

How do we feel when we read a passage such as this? We might feel puzzled or embarrassed or feel totally unconnected to this part of our tradition. One way to feel connected to such information is to see it as a way of connecting with a past era of our people that was, in some ways, quite different from our own. It makes the fact that so much of rabbinic literature is still relevant to our lives even more remarkable when we think that it was produced in a world whose conditions varied so much from ours. [JZA, SAA]

Sickness and Sin

Along with the magic beliefs they had about medicine, the Sages maintained that sin, sickness, and suffering were integrally related. They thought, as we will see, that sin could bring on sickness, but that suffering need not be seen as a punishment from God. That is, righteous persons, as well as evil ones, could be afflicted with illnesses and even die. In addition, they taught that suffering need not be borne gladly. On the other hand, physical suffering could bring spiritual benefits, not just to the sufferer, but to a whole community:

> Rabbi [Yehudah HaNasi] lived in Sepphoris and had a toothache for thirteen years. Rabbi Yose, the son of Rabbi Bun, said, "For all those thirteen years a wild animal did not die in the Land of Israel, nor did a pregnant woman miscarry there." And why was he afflicted with this toothache? One time, as he was passing by, he saw a calf about to be slaughtered. It cried out and said to him, "Rabbi, save me." He said to it, "For this you were created." And in the end how was [the tooth] cured? They saw [people] about to kill a nest of mice, [and Rabbi] said, "Let them be, [for] it is written, 'And His compassion is over all that He has made'" (Psalm 145:9). (*Y. Kilayim* 9:3, 32b)

This story attributes healing powers to the suffering of one great man, Rabbi Yehudah HaNasi, who compiled the Mishnah in approximately 200 C.E. He is afflicted with this suffering because he refused to show mercy to a calf. He is only cured when he shows mercy to animals that are regarded as pests and urges that they not be killed. During the years that he suffered, wild animals in the Land of Israel did not die, nor did women have miscarriages. In other words, others were relieved of suffering through his suffering. Sin, suffering, and the health of every Jew are interconnected in this story, as they often are in rabbinic literature. Another legend relates that a small infraction of Jewish principles could result in sickness.

It is related of Nahum of Gamzu that he was blinded in both his eyes, his two hands and legs were amputated, and his whole body was covered with boils and he was lying in a dilapidated house on a bed the feet of which were standing in bowls of water in order to prevent the ants from crawling on to him. . . . His disciples said to him, Master, since you are wholly righteous, why has all this befallen you? And he replied, I have brought it all upon myself. Once I was journeying on the road and was making for the house of my father-in-law and I had with me three asses, one laden with food, one with drink and one with all kinds of dainties, when a poor man met me and stopped me on the road and said to me, Master, give me something to eat. I replied to him, Wait until I have unloaded something from the ass; I had hardly managed to unload something from the ass when the man died [from hunger]. I then went and laid myself on him and exclaimed, May my eyes which had no pity upon your eyes become blind, may my hands which had no pity upon your hands be cut off, may my legs which had no pity upon your legs be amputated, and my mind was not at rest until I added, may my whole body be covered with boils. Thereupon his pupils exclaimed, Alas that we see you in such sore plight. To this he replied, Woe would it be to me did you not see me in such a sore plight. Why was he called Nahum of Gamzu? Because whatever befell him he would declare, This is also for the best. (*B. Taanit* 21a)

Strictly speaking, Nahum does not break Jewish law. He simply is not quick enough in providing the requested charity. For this, he curses himself with blindness, lameness, and boils. Such suffering was often understood as a chastisement of love, that is, a burden from God that, if bravely born, would result in rewards during life after death. As we can see, there is little division, if any, for the Sages among the spiritual, physical, and psychological realms.

Samuel: The Maimonides of Rabbinic Literature

Perhaps the best-known person who was both a rabbi and a physician was Maimonides. He lived from 1135 to 1204 C.E., which is long past the period of works we are considering in this book. However, there was one Sage of the rabbinic era who, like Maimonides, was both a rabbi and a physician. This Sage, Samuel, was an expert in pediatrics and was also knowledgeable about astronomy. He was born about 180 C.E. in Nehardea, Babylonia, and died there in 257.

In ancient days, as today, good physicians were respected and generally held in high esteem. For example, Samuel once acted as Rabbi Yehudah HaNasi's physician and cured him of an eye ailment so gently and effectively that the latter wanted to bestow the title "Rabbi" on him (*B. Baba Metsia* 85b–86a). However, Samuel never received this honorific title and is referred to by the slightly less flattering title *Mar*, which means "master."

Mar Samuel was renowned in Babylonia as a teacher of religious knowledge, as well as a medical expert. He was wealthy and had many contacts among the ruling

Jewish and non-Jewish authorities (e.g., *Y. Taanit* 4:2, 68a). He was also a well-respected judge of a Jewish court and is the source of the famous edict "The law of the land is the law" (*B. Baba Kamma* 113b), which is observed to this day. Thus, for example, American Jews are required by this principle to observe all the secular laws of the United States, as well as to keep Jewish traditions.

Mar Samuel's medical experience is entwined with his knowledge of Torah. For example, he likens Torah to breast-feeding:

> "Her breasts will satisfy you at all times" (Proverbs 5:19). Why were the words of the Torah compared to a breast? As with a breast, however often the child sucks he finds milk in it, so it is with the words of the Torah. As often as a person studies them so often does he find something tasty in them. (*B. Eruvin* 54b)

In the verse from Proverbs, Wisdom (i.e., Torah) is personified as a woman and is seen as a nurturing, loving presence. Mar Samuel specifically comments on the part of the verse regarding breasts and relates it to something he may have seen as a physician: a mother produces milk to meet her child's needs and Torah, like a caring, nursing mother, can provide us with what we need to grow spiritually. In such ways, Mar Samuel represents an excellent blend and balance of Jewish and scientific knowledge, piety and practicality.

Physicians and Rabbis

It is interesting that the dual career of rabbi (or scholar) and physician is a common one throughout Jewish history. Harry Friedenwald notes this close connection and suggests it is related to the high esteem with which Jews have often regarded physicians. He states, "The rabbi-physician chose the practice of medicine not only as a means of livelihood but as a favorite occupation because of the opportunity it afforded to devote one's life to good deeds and to become the instrument of Providence to bring relief."[6] In addition, it also happens that the Sages frequently needed to work at a trade or profession in order to make a living.

> Nowadays this combination might tax even the most supportive parents' resources. For example, allowing 5 years for rabbinical school, 4 years for medical school, 3 years for pediatric residency, and 3 years for neonatal fellowship, it would take at least 15 years after college for a person to be prepared to be both a rabbi and a neonatologist. Far easier for a rabbi to marry a neonatologist. . . .[SAA]

Abaye's Nurse:
A Great Teacher of Medical Knowledge

We could not talk about great teachers of medicine in rabbinic literature without mentioning a nameless, but very influential, teacher: Abaye's nurse. Abaye was a great Babylonian Sage who taught between 280 and 338 C.E. He was raised by a woman he calls his nurse or simply "mother." We learn elsewhere, however, that she is not his biological mother:

> Rabbi Johanan said: Happy is he who has not seen them [his father and mother since the commandment to honor

one's parents is so difficult to fulfill]. Rabbi Johanan's father died when his mother conceived him, and his mother died when she bore him. And Abaye was likewise. But this is not so, for Abaye said, "My Mother told me!" That was his foster mother. (*B. Kiddushin* 31b)

This passage examines how difficult it is to fully observe the commandment to honor one's father and mother. It is in this connection that Rabbi Johanan says that those who are orphaned from birth are fortunate, for they do not have to attempt to observe this commandment. Apparently, both Rabbi Johanan and Abaye were orphaned from birth and so were exempt from observing this mitzvah, this precept. There is a bit of confusion about Abaye's orphaned state, because he frequently quotes someone he calls his "mother." However, it is made clear in the passage above that this woman is really his foster mother, not his biological mother.

Abaye's foster mother was apparently quite an expert in child care and in the medical knowledge of her day, for Abaye frequently quotes her as his source of medical information. Her teachings tell us about medicine as it was practiced in that era. In addition, they show us that this woman, and possibly others, played a large role in practicing and teaching medicine.

Other Ancient Physicians

Hippocrates (460–370 B.C.E.) is usually credited with establishing much of the scientific basis of medicine. He did not write specific treatises on pediatric diseases, but he repeatedly referred to the special features of childhood diseases. For example, he believed that children were afflicted with tapeworms *in utero.*

> Tapeworms, I claim, are produced in the child while yet *in utero,* for after leaving the uterus feces never remain in the bowel long enough for an animal of such size to be formed from the putrefaction and decay of feces in the intestine.[7]

As we begin to consider medical history, this passage can serve to remind us how little the ancients had to go on, and how much they had to guess how things occurred. Tapeworms are not acquired *in utero,* but usually from eating infected food, such as meat. Today they can be treated with medication (anti-helminithics).

An interesting but nearly tragic story related to this teaching was a recent outbreak within the Orthodox Jewish community of New York of the pork tapeworm *Taenia solium,* which causes the disease cysticercosis. In a few children, the disease led to severe symptoms, including seizures. Needless to say, this disease was among the last diagnoses considered since usually one must eat uncooked pork to acquire it. On careful investigation, it turned out that the tapeworm was introduced into the households by the families' domestic employees who had recently emigrated from another country. The unusual nature of this outbreak was so compelling that it was published in the prestigious *New England Journal of Medicine,* presumably as an example of the importance of considering any possibility in arriving at a medical diagnosis. Fortunately, the article indicates that complete, or near complete, recovery was achieved by the children affected.[8]

Soranus's Classic Textbook *Gynecology*

Another source of great importance to our understanding of ancient obstetrics and infant care is the work of the Greek physician Soranus. He lived in the second century c.e., during the time when rabbinic literature was being written. Since he was a contemporary of the Sages, and is one of the principal ancient authorities on obstetric and infant care, comparisons between his writings and those of the Sages help put the latter in an appropriate historical context.

Soranus studied in Alexandria and then practiced medicine in Rome between 98 and 138 c.e. He wrote a work entitled *Gynecology*, which, despite its title, is a thorough description of both the fields of obstetrics and gynecology and newborn care. Soranus provides remarkably clear explanations of medical conditions and was an astute observer. For example, he describes in detail methods for evaluating a mother's milk based on its color, smell, density, and so forth, to ensure that the milk would be healthy for a baby. These methods were used for many centuries. They can even be found in eighteenth-century medical texts and are the forerunner of modern methods of analyzing milk composition.

The Physician in Ancient Society and the Modern Physician

Some things are constant. One of those constants is that people often have deep and ambivalent feelings regarding their physicians. For example, in the Mishnah we learn the following:

The best physician deserves *Gehenna* (Hell). (*M. Kid-dushin* 4:14)

.

This statement comes as part of a general discussion about the merits of different occupations. In addition, we learn there that ass drivers are mostly wicked men and sailors mostly pious ones. Obviously, physicians were not well thought of by Rabbi Judah, who states these opinions. Rashi, in his commentary on this passage (*B. Kiddushin* 82a), explains this statement in several ways. It could refer to the fact that even very good physicians frequently cause tremendous harm to innocent people. In addition, physicians are blamed for being overconfident, that is, trusting in their own skills instead of in God to heal the patient. They may also commercialize their profession and neglect the needs of poor persons.

Others say it is because a physician despairs of a patient whose cure will take too much time and thereby causes the patient's death.[9] The physician might not express all of her knowledge and profess not to know a disease or its cure if she does not desire to treat a patient. Steinsaltz suggests that another way a physician could merit *Gehenna* is by failing to offer treatment in a timely manner and thereby cause a person's death. Finally, another suggested explanation is that a truly good physician, who is quite honest, would convey to patients that their situations are hopeless and in this way merit *Gehenna*. Perhaps this statement in the Mishnah reflects the fact that every physician, no matter how talented and honest, is defeated by death. In addition, it reflects the danger that physicians may see themselves as superhuman when they temporarily banish death and that they may not practice their craft in humility and charity.

Ambivalence toward physicians remains a significant part of our current view of medicine. On the one hand, we continue to honor physicians: few parents would . object to their child attending medical school. On the other hand, physicians increasingly shoulder the blame for the ills of modern medicine. It is time we moved beyond this love–hate relationship to examine the true issues facing modern medicine, such as the inadequate health care received by many underprivileged children in America. For example, currently a majority of inner-city toddlers are not immunized on time. [SAA, JZA]

Having learned all these negative lessons about physicians, our tradition turns around and, in commenting on this mishnah, the Yerushalmi states a quite different attitude:

It is forbidden to live in a city where there is no physician, no bath and no court administering floggings and imprisoning people. Said Rabbi Yose son of Rabbi Bun, "Also it is forbidden to live in a town in which there is no vegetable garden." Rabbi Hezekiah, Rabbi Kohen in the name of Rav: "In the future a person is going to have to give an account of himself for everything that his eye saw and he did not eat." (*Y. Kiddushin* 4:12, 66d)

Interestingly, this teaching about the value of physicians is paired with prohibitions against living in towns without baths, courts of law (which can punish wrongdoers), and vegetable gardens, as well as a teaching that urges us to eat and enjoy life when we have the opportunity to do so. These, it seems, are the basic requirements for keeping out of harm's way: proper medical care, a means for maintaining personal hygiene, a system to control people's behavior, a reliable source of healthy food, and a healthy mental attitude, which allows for the enjoyment of that food. To put it another way, it is not wise to live in a town that has no medical care, water and sewer system, police and courts, and a grocery store. These are basic necessities for maintaining a healthy and orderly life.

Another feature of medical practice that has remained constant over the centuries is that physicians charge a fee for the medical care they provide, and that this is expected and proper.

> A physician who takes no fee is worth no fee. (B. *Baba Kamma* 85a)

This statement comes up in an exchange between an injured person and the one who inflicted the injury. The latter must provide medical care and other compensation to the former and, as a way of saving money, offers to bring a physician who charges nothing for her healing art. The retort by the injured party is, "A physician who charges nothing is worth nothing." Today, this concept still frequently holds true (charity care excepted). Physicians are expected to bill their patients regardless of the outcome. And people are often quite willing to pay great sums of money to famous specialists and may be wary of going to physicians who charge very little.

Modern Authorities on Judaism and Medicine

No work on medicine and rabbinic literature could fail to take account of Julius Preuss's classic text *Biblical and*

Talmudic Medicine.[10] It was Preuss, an expert in both rabbinic literature and medicine, who provided the first systematic, comprehensive study of medicine in rabbinic literature. In particular, he sorts out, in great detail, the large number of diseases described in the Bible and rabbinic literature and attempts to determine their modern equivalents. For example, he demonstrates that the disease referred to as leprosy in the Bible may have included many different illnesses. His book, though completed in 1886, is still the authoritative work on the subject today.

Our book does not in any way attempt to replace Preuss's work. Rather, we hope to provide the reader with specific passages from rabbinic literature that are relevant to pediatrics and place them in both their historical and modern contexts. In particular, we dwell on those passages from rabbinic literature that feature the insights of the Sages into child care and that can best help parents raise their children, both Jewishly and medically.

The Modern History of Pediatrics

The specialty of pediatrics is a relatively new one. Pediatrics as a specialized branch of medicine had no real existence before the middle of the nineteenth century, when children's hospitals first began to appear in the United States.

I work in the subspecialty neonatology, which did not even exist in a meaningful way when I was born (1957). The term neonatology was not used until 1960. Neonatologists are pediatricians who specialize in the care of newborn infants and especially infants born prematurely.

In addition to practicing clinical neonatology, I spend much of my time doing research on the nutritional needs of children. Specifically, my research focuses on evaluating the best ways to provide calcium and other minerals to infants and older older children to enhance the development of strong bones. [SAA]

The incredible changes that have developed in the care of newborn infants during the past 30 years make it easy to lose one's perspective. Medical care for sick newborns is an intense, highly technological specialty. It has placed both doctors and families at the edge of difficult personal and ethical dilemmas that frequently spill over into the newspapers and the courts.

3

The Importance
of Children in
the Jewish Tradition

We begin our discussion with the most basic of questions: What is the place of the child in Judaism? It should surprise no one at all familiar with the Jewish faith and culture that children are accorded the highest importance in rabbinic literature. A religion that relies so strongly on the continuation of generation after generation to transmit its message will naturally value children, and what they learn and do, to a great extent.

The Importance of Children to God

Our Sages taught that God pays careful attention to our children. Even before birth, God empowers them with special abilities to understand the world and learn Torah.

[During the period of gestation] a light burns above the fetus' head, and it gazes and is able to see from one end of the world to the other. . . . There is no time during which a person abides in greater happiness than during those days. . . . It is taught the entire Torah, all of it. . . . But as it comes into the air of the world, an angel comes, strikes it on its mouth, and makes it forget the entire Torah. (*B. Niddah* 30b)

In this passage, the Sages may be reflecting what most parents feel when they see and hold their children for the first time: here is a bit of clay, enlivened by God; a piece of perfection, of innocence, of the Divine. The Sages felt the best way to express this was to relate it to the feelings of awe, respect, and love we feel toward the Torah. Just as we treat a Torah scroll gently and hold it reverently, so do we hold and treat a child with love and reverence. In addition, this passage reflects that a child's time *in utero* is the happiest in his life. His needs are met automatically, and his environment is constant and comfortable. The Sages cannot imagine such a complete and perfect existence without Torah, so they assume that the child has learned it all while in the womb.

The Sages also felt that young children, even fetuses, were highly valued individuals who could participate in Jewish history. For example, children were integrally involved at the parting of the Red Sea:

Our Rabbis taught: Rabbi Yose HaGalillee expounded: At the time the Israelites ascended from the Red Sea, they desired to utter a song; and how did they render the song? The babe lay upon his mother's knee and the suckling nursed at his mother's breast; when they beheld the *Shekhinah* (God's presence), the babe raised his neck and the suckling released the nipple from his mouth, and they exclaimed, "This is my God and I will praise Him" (Exodus 15:3); as it is said, "Out of the mouths of babes and sucklings have You established strength" (Psalm 8:3).

Rabbi Meir used to say, Whence is it that even the fetuses in their mothers' womb uttered a song [as the Red Sea parted]? As it is said "Bless you the Lord in the congregation, even the Lord, from the fountain of Israel" (Psalm 68:27). But these [fetuses] could not behold [the *Shekhinah*]? Rabbi Tanhum said: The abdomen became for them a kind of transparent medium and they did behold it. (*B. Sotah* 30b–31a)

When the Israelites were rescued at the Red Sea by God's presence (called the *Shekhinah*), they sang a triumphant song (Exodus 15:1–18). In this passage, we learn that God's presence is so magnificent and overpowering that young children—even fetuses—were aware of it and sang part of the song: "This is my God and I will praise Him" (Exodus 15:3). The verse from Psalm 68 is taken as proof that the fetuses sang because the woman's womb is often likened to a fountain, which is mentioned as the place from whence a song of praise comes.

It is tempting to regard this passage as simply a fanciful interpretation of an important, all-encompassing moment in Jewish history. However, we might stop and ask, "What can the fetus learn and when?" This is a matter of some controversy and a considerable amount of research. It has been reported that in the last few weeks of pregnancy the fetus can hear and responds to loud sounds by changing its heart rate. One research group used changes in sucking patterns to demonstrate that within the first 3 days of life infants could be shown to recognize their mother's voice. It has also been reported that newborns preferentially responded to a story that had been read to them repeatedly prenatally. In one report, a group of British infants in the first week of life whose mothers had watched a particular soap opera while they were pregnant quit crying or changed their level of alertness when the show came on, whereas other infants whose mothers had not watched the "show" were unaffected. The validity and interpretation of these studies remain uncertain, but they are consistent with the traditional Jewish views of fetal learning.

> *Whether it is a good idea for infants to recognize soap opera theme music has not been evaluated.*
>
> *Children respond to repetition and patterns once they're out of the womb, too. When I was in rabbinical school I attended daily services at a synagogue in the area. One of the rabbis who worked there would bring his 2-year-old son with him every day. The father would make his way down the center aisle, shaking hands and briefly greeting each person, and the son did the same, solemnly shaking each person's hands and then moving on. It was a heartwarming way to begin services (which, of course, the boy already knew by heart). It could be argued, what good is it for him to know the order of the service if he didn't know what it meant? Not only was it valuable for the boy to know the structure so he could eventually come to understand its content more easily, but surely God takes pleasure from hearing prayers sung by such small voices.*
>
> *Indeed, if we are created in God's image, then we can see a hint of God's reaction as parents watch their children pray. At our Consecration services, when we welcome children beginning their religious educations, the consecrants sing the Shema as a class and,*

*in general, the parents are obviously filled with joy
and gratification.* [SAA, JZA]

To Be Fruitful and Multiply

The important role of Jewish children in their families is
the subject of many stories and teachings in rabbinic literature. Beginning with the Torah's command to "be fruitful and multiply" (Genesis 1:28), and unaltered today, is
a firm sense of the value of children to ourselves and to
Judaism. For example, we are commanded in the stron-
gest terms to marry and have children:

> Rabbi Eliezer stated, He who does not engage in propa-
> gation of the race is as though he sheds blood; for it is
> said, "Whoever sheds man's blood by man shall his blood
> be shed" (Genesis 9:6) and this is immediately followed
> by the text, "And you, be fruitful and multiply" (Genesis
> 9:7). Rabbi Eleazar ben Azariah said: [Whoever sheds
> blood it is] as though he diminished the Divine Image.
> (*B. Yebamot* 63b)

As we will see many times, the Sages believed that everything in the Bible is done purposefully and deliberately.
So the juxtaposition of two verses is seen as having meaning behind it. In this case, God, laying down the ground
rules for Noah as he is about to leave the ark and begin
civilization anew, tells Noah:

> Whoso sheds man's blood, by man shall his blood be
> shed, for in the image of God made He man. And you,
> be you fruitful and multiply; swarm in the earth, and mul-
> tiply therein. (Genesis 9:6–7)

God decries bloodshed in Genesis 9:6, outlining how
Divine justice will work, and in the very next verse com-
mands Noah and his children to be fruitful and multiply.
The Sages assume that these two verses are placed together for a reason, which they deduce to be that if one
does not have children, it is as if that person has shed
blood. Because God's image is also mentioned in this
connection, Rabbi Eleazar ben Azariah also says that one
who does not have children is like one who diminishes
God's image in the world. Of course, it could be said that
the Sages were predisposed to see these messages in the
text, for they considered having and raising children to
be of utmost importance.

*It is unfortunate that so many stories in the media
about parents are about those who abuse or abandon
their children. In general, most parents passionately
care about their children and invest enormous amounts
of energy and emotion in their development and well-
being. At my congregation, during* bar *and* bat mitzvah *ceremonies, the parents address the child, expressing their pride and joy. When the parents start crying
(almost all of them do), they express embarrassment,
as if this were somehow abnormal. On the contrary,
this is the most normal thing in the world. Those feelings of pride and gratification, of holding on and letting go at the same time, are what make parenthood
so precious.* [JZA]

Having and Caring for Children

The Sages were a practical group of men. They realized
that Judaism is a religion that is lived in the physical world,

and so the physical world is holy. Given this mindset, it is easy to see how the Sages valued health and children as a part of holiness.

> Seven are banned by Heaven, and these are they: a Jew who has no wife; he who has a wife but no children; and he who has children but does not bring them up to the study of the Torah; and he who has no phylacteries (*tefillin*) on his head and on his arm, no fringes on his garment and no *mezuzah* on his door, and he who denies his feet shoes. (*B. Pesachim* 113b)

First we note that all seven of these desirable behaviors are physical in nature. Judaism is a religion that does not deny the body and its needs, but places them in a context of holiness. These are the prerequisites for entering Heaven, according to the Sages. We can express these ideas in the following, positive, way. One must be married and have children who are brought up to study Torah. One must publicly proclaim God's oneness by wearing *tefillin* (black leather boxes containing verses from Scriptures that are attached to the head and hand). Though today they are normally worn only during morning worship services, in the rabbinic era they were worn all day long, thus proclaiming that one was a faithful Jew. Likewise, one must wear *tsitsit*, the fringes that remind us to do *mitzvot* (God's commandments), and by having a *mezuzah*, verses from Scripture attached to one's door, which proclaims that one's home is Jewish. And finally, one must take care of one's health and safety, that is, value the life given us by God (wearing shoes was considered protection against scorpion bites and other common hazards in the ancient Near East). Having children, and raising them, ranks right up there with having faith in one God and preserving one's own life. That's how important raising children is to the Sages. What is the logic behind this list? It describes a person who is healthy physically, emotionally, and spiritually. Someone who does these seven things not only takes care of himself, but is also devoted to those things that sustain the Jewish people and are ultimately greater than any individual. This passage seems to indicate that we have to take care of ourselves, be connected to others, and be connected to God, to be whole as persons.

Generation to Generation:
Grandparents and Grandchildren

Though we will be addressing issues of parenting and pediatrics in this book, we cannot help but say a word about the role grandparents play in children's lives. We note that doting grandparents are nothing new in Judaism, as we learn from the Bible:

Grandchildren are the crown of old men. (Proverbs 17:6)

According to reliable reports, the satisfaction of relating to one's grandchildren is beyond compare. There is a freedom and preciousness in that relationship that in some ways surpasses the bond between parent and child. Today, particularly in families where one parent does not have a Jewish education, grandparents can play a significant role in helping their grandchildren learn about Judaism. The value of tutelage by a grandparent was apparent even in the days of the Sages.

Now is the grandfather under this obligation [to teach his grandson Torah]? . . . Rabbi Joshua ben Levi said: He who teaches his grandson Torah, Scripture regards him as though he had received it [direct] from Mount Sinai, for it is said, "and you shall make them known unto your children and your children's children" (Deuteronomy 4:9), which is followed by, "that is the day that you stood before the Lord your God in Horeb" (Deuteronomy 4:10). (B. Kiddushin 30a)

The Sages are once more commenting on the juxtaposition of two verses and deducing the reason they are put together. The two verses from Deuteronomy read as follows:

Only take heed to yourself, and keep your soul diligently, lest you forget the things which your eyes saw, and lest they depart from your heart all the days of your life; but make them known unto your children and your children's children. The day that you stood before the Lord your God in Horeb [Mount Sinai], when the Lord said unto me: "Assemble Me the people, and I will make them hear My words that they may learn to fear Me all the days that they live upon the earth, and that they may teach their children." (Deuteronomy 4:9–10)

The Sages wonder what these two verses, one about teaching one's grandchildren and the other about standing at Mount Sinai and receiving the law, have to do with one another. The answer is that when one is teaching one's grandchildren Torah, the moment of revelation on Mount Sinai is recreated. We even have a story about a Sage who took this lesson to heart so seriously that he transgressed a rule of halakhah, Jewish law, in order to teach his grandson.

Every Friday afternoon, Rabbi Joshua ben Levi regularly
listened to his grandson's reading of the Scripture lesson
[studied during the week]. Once, he forgot to do so, and,
when he had already entered the baths of Tiberias, lean-
ing on the shoulder of R. Hiyya bar Ba, he remembered
that he had not listened to his grandson's reading of Scripture while he was in the bath and he went out of the bath
. . . R. Hiyya bar Ba said to him: Did not Rabbi [Yehudah
HaNasi] teach us that if one has begun [taking a bath],
one may not interrupt [even for prayer, *M. Shabbat* 1:2]?
Rabbi Joshua said to him, "Hiyya, my son, is it a small
matter to you that he who listens to his grandson's reading of Scripture is as though he were hearing it at Mount
Sinai? For it is said, 'Make them known unto your children and your children's children, as if it were the day that
you stood before the Lord Your God in Horeb'" (Deuteronomy 4:9–10). (*Y. Shabbat* 1:2, 3a)

Bathing was considered a meritorious activity by the
Sages: it kept one healthy and clean (see, e.g., *Leviticus
Rabbah* 34:3). Sages were strongly discouraged from
living in a town that did not have a public bath (*B.
Sanhedrin* 17b). These public baths could be luxurious,
with pools of hot, warm, and cold water for the bathers
(*B. Shabbat* 40a). The Sages ruled (*M. Shabbat* 1:2) that
a person should not begin an activity such as bathing or
getting a haircut around the time when afternoon prayers
are to be said until he has said those prayers. However, if
the person has begun such an activity, he can put off
saying the afternoon service until he has finished the bath
or the haircut. (Today, some men still go to the *mikveh*,
a public ritual bath, before *Shabbat* begins.)
    We can imagine the Sages preparing for the Sabbath

by bathing, so that they should be clean and relaxed, when all of a sudden, one of them runs out to listen to his grandson's lesson. How does Rabbi Joshua explain this breach of etiquette? He tells his colleague that it is more important to him to listen to his grandson's lesson than to socialize with his friends, to conform to the Sages' code of etiquette, or even to be clean for *Shabbat*. In other words, he puts the re-creation of the moment of revelation at Sinai—and his relationship with his grandson—above all these other values. This value system will often be reflected in the texts we will explore. The Sages placed the education and well-being of children above almost any other competing value.

Grandparents can be a great source of Jewish memories, knowledge, and inspiration. Whether these lessons are taught through dramatic stories of Jewish life in Europe or through the Jewish history of one's own town, they are sure to delight grandchildren who want to know where their families came from. In addition, when grandparents express their own pride in their grandchildren's Jewish competency, they reinforce parental pride and demonstrate in a different and important way that the child's Jewishness is important to those who love him. [JZA, SAA]

God's Mercy and Children

Our schoolchildren are central not only to the future of the Jewish people but even to the existence of the cosmos. According to the Sages, they play a vital role in maintaining the Universe.

Every day an angel goes forth from before the Holy One,
blessed be He, to destroy the world and make it revert to
its original [chaos], but when the Holy One, blessed be
He, looks upon the school children at their school house
and scholars who sit in their Houses of Study His anger
immediately turns to mercy. (*Kallah Rabbati* 2:9)

When our children—and we—study Torah, we create
mercy, as it were. The study of Torah leads to a life of
good deeds, a life that is more readily and fully lived in
accordance with God's will, and such a life redeems the
Universe. Passages from rabbinic literature like this one,
which appear fanciful on the surface, often turn out to be
quite realistic once we delve into their logic.

*How can we, as parents, turn the love of our children
into mercy? By understanding our own families of
origin and working through whatever problems we
had in them and by making spiritual journeys that
ensure that we develop and grow in understanding
and wisdom. We may not be able to avoid making
mistakes as we raise our children, but we owe it to
them, and to ourselves, to at least make different mistakes than our parents made with us and avoid repeat-
ing destructive patterns from our own childhoods.*
[SAA, JZA]

Concluding Thoughts

How often do we look into our children's faces and see
there the most important thing in our lives? Is this merely
a cultural attitude or is it a deeper, religious value that
expresses a key message of Judaism? What does it say

about our faith that, because children are so important, celibacy was never condoned as a main form of religious expression? All these things point to one central truth: raising children is important, not only for the physical continuation of our people, but as a spiritual experience for both parents and children.

II

Childhood Stages

4

Conception and Pregnancy

The Sages saw in children the embodiment of the continuity of the generations. But they expressed some puzzlement that such an important part of life could begin with so potentially sinful an act as sexual intercourse. They wondered what was happening as the mother's belly swelled and why some pregnancies failed and others went easily. Why were some children born whole and well and others born deformed and ill?

We begin our journey through the life cycle of children with an examination of rabbinic beliefs about conception, pregnancy, and childbirth. The Sages' questions about these issues are, in many cases, remarkably similar to questions asked by modern medicine. The answers they deduced were based on what medical knowledge was available at the time, as well as their perceptions of justice and morality. We are still faced with many of the same moral issues, in some cases made more acute by modern technology. The Sages' solutions to these issue can provide us with insight and comfort today.

Conception and Cooperation between God and Parents

The Sages believed that God plays a role in every facet of human functioning. Conception was no exception to that rule. Indeed, God plays an exceedingly important role in the formation of every human person:

> Usually, if a man has given into another's keeping an ounce of silver in private, and the latter returns to him a pound of gold in public, the former will surely be grateful to the latter; even so it is with the Holy One, blessed be He. Human beings entrust to Him a drop of fluid in privacy, and the Holy One, blessed be He, openly returns to them completely perfected individuals. (*Leviticus Rabbah*, *Tazria* 14:2)

The Sages felt that children are created only in partnership with God. Human beings contribute specks of material (egg and semen) that develop, through God's agency, into a full person.

The following passage reiterates the position of the midrashic quotation, above, with some additional refinements:

> Our Rabbis taught: There are three partners in [making] a person, the Holy One, blessed be He, his father and his mother. His father supplies the semen of the white substance out of which are formed the child's bones, sinews,

nails, the brain in his head and the white in his eye; his mother supplies the semen of the red substance out of which is formed his skin, flesh, hair, blood and the black of the eye; and the Holy One, blessed be He, gives him spirit (*ruah*) and soul (*n'shamah*), beauty of features, eyesight and the power of hearing, and the ability to speak and to walk, understanding and discernment. When his time to depart from the world approaches, the Holy One, blessed be He, takes away His share and leaves the shares of his father and mother with them. (*B. Niddah* 31a)

This passage links each gender's "output" with their part of conception. Men emit semen, which is "white," and therefore the Sages attributed to men the formation of the white substances of a person. Women emit menstrual blood, and thus they are associated with the red substances of a person. However, it is God who enlivens the physical body and to whom the faculties are ascribed. Human beings, formed from clay, can only create more clay; more lifeless physicalness. It is God who transforms the clay, the physical, into a human being.

This passage from *B. Niddah* also offers us some insight into the way the Sages saw the aging process. As we age, we lose some of our senses, such as eyesight and hearing. The Sages suggest that growing older and approaching death represent a return of God to reclaim the gifts God gave us.

Though we may not think of what we give our children in terms of "red" and "white" substances, certainly we fantasize, from the moment we read that positive pregnancy test, about seeing ourselves in our children. One of the greatest joys of parenthood is

*laughing with recognition when our children do some-
thing that is so typically "us." This is also a great blessing, for it gives us patience and understanding for
behavior that might otherwise be greeted with impa-
tience. For example, our 2-year-old daughter can concentrate quite fiercely on any game she is playing and
will brook no interruption until it is finished to her
satisfaction. What some other person might see as
stubbornness or rigidity we rejoice in as determination and stick-to-itiveness, qualities we share with her.*
[JZA, SAA]

Choosing Your Child's Gender:
The Sages' View

The command "Be fruitful and multiply" (Genesis 9:7) is
considered to be a great *mitzvah*, a central precept, in
Judaism. One tendency we see quite frequently in rabbinic literature is the propensity to quantify *mitzvot* and
moral concepts. Therefore, it is natural that the Sages ask,
"When has a man [this duty was deemed to devolve only
on men] fulfilled the duty to be fruitful and multiply? How
many children must he have?" The answer, that is, Jewish law, will necessarily define a minimum standard, not
the desired norm. In other words, the Sages wanted people
to have as many children as possible, but they could only
legislate the minimum requirements for fulfilling this *mitzvah*.

A person may not abstain from [the duty to be] fruitful
and multiply unless he already has children. Beit Shammai says, Two male children; and Beit Hillel says, A male
and a female child. (*M. Yebamot* 6:6)

The dispute over when a person has fulfilled the duty to be fruitful and multiply focuses on the gender of the offspring. Beit Shammai, the House of Shammai, whose opinions are generally not taken to be the law, rules that one must produce two sons to fulfill the obligation. Beit Hillel, the House of Hillel, on the other hand, opines that one must produce both a son and a daughter, and this becomes the law. This is not surprising. Beit Shammai generally represents the views of the more well-to-do, while Beit Hillel usually represents the lower classes. A rich family could better afford to continue producing offspring in order to meet the "two boys" requirement than could a poor family. Imagine if Jewish law had been decreed in accordance with Beit Shammai: think of the man who only made a meager living who, having had one boy and five girls, had to continue trying to have another boy—not to mention the strain on his wife! ·

We have been advised by a seasoned veteran that going from two children to three means changing from a "man-for-man" defense to a "zone" defense. [SAA, JZA]

Beit Hillel's opinion, which values sons and daughters equally, may have become the law, but many of our sources indicate that the Sages desired male offspring. For example, we learn how one Sage deals with his disappointment with his child's gender.

After a daughter was born to Rabbi Simeon Berabbi he was disappointed. His father [seeking to comfort him] said, "The possibility for further increase has now come into the world." But Bar Kappara said to R. Simeon, "Your father has offered you vain comfort. The fact is, as we have been taught, the world cannot endure without both males and females. Nevertheless, happy is he whose children are males, and alas for him whose children are females." (B. Baba Batra 16b)

The ambivalence of the Sages is phenomenal! On the one hand, this father of a newborn girl, Rabbi Simeon, is disappointed. On the other, the child's grandfather, who is a great Sage, sees in this baby girl the possibility that she will bear children in time and help the Jewish people survive. This consolation is spurned by another Sage who makes the commonsense observation that we need both males and females for the continuation of our people, but who nonetheless thinks it's better to have male children than female children. Apparently, the Sages' rational understanding that we need both males and females was at war with their emotional wishes for more male children than female children.

> I told the obstetrician who performed the ultrasound on what was to be our first child, Michael, that I wanted him to tell us this would be a girl. After all, wouldn't it be easier for a big sister to hold her ground against a younger brother than for a little sister to have to deal with a big brother? Well, our 2-year-old daughter has demonstrated that she's hardly dominated by having a big brother.
> The idea of requiring a child of each gender sounds great until you consider the neonatologist I know (who happens not to be Jewish) who has ten sons and no daughters. [SAA]

The Sages thought that the way one conducted sexual intercourse influenced the gender of the child produced. They use the presumed desire of most people to have sons in order to encourage their own vision of proper sexual intercourse.

> Rabbi Isaac citing Rabbi Ami stated: If the woman emits her semen first she bears a male child; if the man emits his semen first she bears a female child. . . . Now is it within the power of man to increase the number of "sons and sons' sons" (1 Chronicles 8:40)? But the fact is that because they contained themselves during intercourse in order that their wives should emit their semen first so that their children shall be males, Scripture attributes to them the same merit as if they had themselves caused the increase of the number of their sons and sons' sons. . . . One who desires all his children to be males should cohabit twice in succession. (B. Niddah 31a–b)

In the ancient world it was believed that women, like men, had to reach orgasm for conception to take place. Women were thought to have the same organs as men. These organs differed only in that they were inside the body rather than outside it.[1] One by-product of this conceptualization is that the (presumed) desire for male children would encourage the man to ensure the sexual satisfaction of his spouse. Indeed, providing one's wife with sexual pleasure is an important duty of a husband. Here, fulfilling this obligation is linked with what the Sages considered a reward: male offspring.

Choosing Your Child's Gender:
Modern Technology

Some concerns truly are timeless. Most parents even today have strong feelings about the preferred gender of their offspring. The difference is that in ancient days little could actually be done about it. However, today the natural gender ratio of newborns can be changed using new technology. For example, techniques exist to separate male chromosome (XY) containing sperm from female (XX) containing sperm. These techniques are reported to be 70 to 80 percent successful in leading to the birth of a child of either desired gender. Considerable ongoing research in this area is likely to increase the success of these gender selection techniques still further. Of course, this technique requires artificial insemination at considerable expense (among other drawbacks), but recent studies suggest that many couples would avail themselves of such technology. One study conducted among both male and female college students reported that approximately one-third of the over 200 students surveyed indicated they would use gender selection technology. Of these, 78 percent wanted their firstborn to be a son and 22 percent wanted a girl first. In regard to their first two children, 54 percent wanted both to be boys, 42 percent wanted one of each, and 4 percent wanted two girls.[2]

The strong feelings of dismay I have seen parents express in the delivery room when faced with the birth of a child of the "nondesired" gender suggest that if simplified methods of gender selection are developed they may be widely used. [SAA]

One situation in which we might find merit to gender selection techniques is in cases where a family is at high risk for having boys with a severe illness. For example, consider the situation of parents who have had a previous son with the most common type of muscular dystrophy, Duchenne's. It is an X-linked disease, which means that it almost exclusively occurs in boys whose mothers are symptom-free carriers of the disease. Parents with a son with Duchenne's muscular dystrophy might consider using sperm selection techniques to increase the likelihood of a female fetus. This would decrease the likelihood of needing to consider whether to continue the pregnancy if a male fetus was found by prenatal testing to carry the X-linked disease. (In general, half of all males, but not females, whose mothers are carriers of X-linked diseases, like Duchenne's muscular dystrophy, will have the disorder. With modern techniques these fetuses can be identified by prenatal testing.)

A significant concern exists regarding the possibility that some parents would choose to terminate a pregnancy if the fetus was not of the desired gender. Our natural reaction is to believe that few parents would feel strongly enough about a child's gender to abort it on that basis alone. Published data suggests, however, that such abortions do occur. As we are increasingly able to identify a fetus's gender during the first half of pregnancy, such abortions may become more common.

It is tempting to suggest we should simply ban all gender selection technology, except when it may have a specific medical indication. It is, however, unlikely that a change in civil laws will occur in the United States or that the courts will limit this technology. A better alternative is to begin to talk about this problem and make young people aware of the significance of the choices modern technology may offer them. In the process, we might hearken to Beit Hillel's ruling: boys and girls are considered equally desirable as children in the Jewish tradition.

The Timing of Conception

Any discussion of conception and contraception in the Jewish tradition must begin with an understanding of *niddah*, a woman's period of ritual impurity, which is related to her menstrual cycle. Ascertaining a person's state of ritual purity or impurity had important economic and ritual consequences. For example, priests and their family members who were in a state of ritual impurity could not eat *terumah*, food that was donated to them by lay Israelites.

The laws of ritual purity and impurity related to a woman's menstrual cycle are outlined in Leviticus 15:19–31. In biblical law, a woman was considered ritually impure for the 7 days of her menstrual period. On the eighth day, presuming the bleeding had stopped, she would immerse herself in the *mikveh*, the ritual bath, and be considered ritually clean again (Leviticus 15:28–29). Over time, the customary observance of these laws changed, at the impetus of women, we are told (*B. Niddah* 66a): they counted their period of *niddah* as 5 days of bleeding and 7 "clear" days with no emission of blood, for a total of 12 days of ritual impurity during which sexual intercourse was not to take place. At the end of this period, the woman would immerse herself in the *mikveh*, become ritually pure, and be able to have sexual intercourse with her husband. After abstaining from sexual relations for 12 days, we can imagine that intercourse would take place promptly on the twelfth day.

These laws about ritual impurity had great symbolic significance and were applied to men as well as to women. Men who had a seminal emission (e.g., a "wet dream") were also considered in a state of ritual impurity and had to go through purification similar to women after their menstrual periods. What was the symbolic importance of menstrual blood and of seminal fluid emitted without sexual intercourse? These fluids were associated with death: menstrual blood meant there was no pregnancy, and seminal fluid expended outside of sexual intercourse was wasted in terms of procreation. This was yet another symbolic way that the Sages underscored the importance of children: those fluids associated with a lack of children were considered ritually impure. We should understand that neither menstruating women nor men with seminal emissions were perceived as being "dirty." Rather, what struck fear in the Sages was a lack of life, that is, death, and it is death that is considered ritually impure. Therefore, it is not surprising that the most ritually impure object in the Sages' entire system was a corpse. Death was, for them, fearsome and life was holy.

The Sages apparently were not certain of the relationship between segments of the menstrual cycle and conception, as witnessed, for example, in the following passage.

> Rabbi Isaac cited Rabbi Ami: A woman conceives only immediately before her menstrual period . . . but Rabbi Yohanan stated: A woman conceives only immediately after her ritual immersion. (B. Niddah 31b)

Was the length of niddah set so as to optimize fertility? Although this appears to be the case, the presence of both opinions in this text suggests some uncertainty. It may be that the Sages were aware that conception was unlikely during menses or shortly thereafter. Clearly, conception was important to them, but without an understanding of when a woman released her eggs and when the sperm fertilized them, they could only base their rulings on observation and guesswork.

> While we strongly and clearly reject the idea of menstruation and menstrual blood as "dirty" or "defiling," we also recognize that when a couple is trying to get pregnant, the onset of a menstrual period is a source of sadness and disappointment. Depending on how long one has been in the process of trying to conceive a child, it may even be a source of desperation or depression. These feelings probably come closer to describing what is meant by the term tamei, which is translated "ritually impure," than any others. [JZA, SAA]

When the Sages Wanted to Prevent Pregnancy

As we have already mentioned, having children was of utmost importance in the Jewish tradition. However, there were times when the Sages considered contraception appropriate, as outlined in this Toseftan passage:

> Three kinds of women have intercourse with a contraceptive device (mokh): a girl under age, a pregnant woman, and a nursing mother. A girl under age—lest she become pregnant and die. What is a girl under age? From eleven years and one day until twelve years and one day. One younger than that or older than that—one has intercourse in the normal way. Therefore one has intercourse in the normal way and does not scruple. A pregnant woman— lest she make the fetus a sandal (a fish-shaped abortus). A nursing mother—lest she kill her infant. (T. Niddah 2:6)

This passage is one of the most important in rabbinic literature on the subject of birth control. The device it mentions, the *mokh*, is some form of absorbent material to be used either before, during, or after coitus. The *mokh*, which is comparable to "barrier methods" (e.g., contraceptive sponges) used today, was not the only form of contraception known in this era. In addition, sterilizing potions existed (*T. Yebamot* 8:4) and coitus interruptus was also practiced as a means of contraception (Genesis 38:8-9; *B. Yebamot* 34b). Let us examine the first two situations mentioned in this passage in turn. We will deal with the nursing mother in Chapter Six.

Pregnancy and Young Girls

The Sages allow a girl whom they consider able to conceive, but too young to do so safely, to use a contraceptive device. The Sages were apparently concerned that pregnancy could be harmful or fatal to an 11- or 12-year-old girl. Intercourse with a girl younger than 11 years old was permitted without contraceptives since they believed there was no fear of conception. Currently, the average age for reaching menarche is about 12½ years. Soranus suggests it was about 13 or 14 years of age in ancient times. Therefore, concerns about an 11-year-old becoming pregnant may have been more theoretical than real in most cases and may have represented the Sages' overall concern about betrothal at such an early age. Although rare, conception prior to 11 years of age has been described.

The effects of pregnancy and childbirth on a young girl's health can be quite serious. Recent studies document an increased risk to mother and baby from pregnancy occurring prior to 15 years of age. Today, we might wonder why the Sages permitted marriage for such a young girl, especially since it appears that both they and the Greeks were aware that this might involve health risks for her. In general, the Sages favored early marriages for both males and females, perhaps due to high mortality rates in early adulthood. In other words, if life expectancy was 25 years, then 13 was middle age.

> While we will more fully discuss teenage sexual activity and contraception in Chapter Nine, this might be a good time to point out that Judaism rarely holds one value supreme without relating it to other values. For example, telling the truth is important, but sometimes shading the truth in order to spare someone's feelings is more important. So, too, children are important but there are times when pregnancy is not a good thing, and Judaism recognizes this. [SAA, JZA]

One Baby, Many Fathers?

Our Toseftan passage also allows a pregnant woman to use a *mokh*. Why? Because the Sages believed that a pregnant woman could conceive again and that the first fetus would be crushed by the second fetus and become a *sandal*. The concern about pregnancy in an already pregnant woman may be related to the ancient belief in superfecundation, that is, that one fetus can have the genetic inheritance of more than one father. The Sages express many points of view on this topic, and the following passage is an example of their argumentational style:

You may further derive that a woman [may] become pregnant and go and become pregnant again [prior to delivering the first fetus].

You may further derive that a woman cannot become pregnant from two [different] men simultaneously.

Now this view differs from that of the rabbis of the field of biblical lore, for rabbis of the field of biblical lore say, "'Behold the champion, the Philistine of Gath, Goliath by name, came up out of the ranks of the Philistines (1 Samuel 17:23).' He was the son of a hundred different Philistine fathers (literally, one hundred Philistine foreskins), who had had sexual relations [with his mother]."

Said Rabbi Mattenaiah, "They do not in fact differ. Before the semen putrefies, a woman may become pregnant from two men simultaneously. But once the semen putrefies, a woman cannot become pregnant from two men simultaneously." (Y. Yebamot 4:2, 5c–d)

Here we see the Sages' opposing views about this issue. On the one hand, some Sages believed that a woman could not become pregnant from two men simultaneously. On the other hand, they had a tradition from the Rabanan d'agad'ta, the Rabbis who tell stories related to the Bible, that Goliath's great strength derived from the fact that he was fathered by a hundred men. They derived this teaching from a play on words, a pun. In the Bible, there is a difference between the way the word "ranks of Philistines" is written and the way it is actually read. It is read mima'arkhot Plishtim but is written mima'arot Plishtim, and the way it is written is extremely similar to the words mimei'ah orlot Plishtim, "from 100 foreskins of Philistines," that is, from a hundred Philistine fathers. This midrash thus suggests that the Sages believed that many men can father one child.

Rabbi Mattenaiah reconciles these two teachings by introducing the factor of timing, relying on the principle, seen elsewhere (e.g., *B. Berachot* 60a), that the semen does not putrefy for 3 days and that therefore if a woman has intercourse with two men within that 3-day period they could each contribute to a single fetus, being a "part-father." The ancients believed that it was possible during early pregnancy for a second father to mix his semen with the previous man's and create one fetus with characteristics of both men. These beliefs persisted until relatively recent times, when the characteristics of sperm and egg were more clearly understood.

Modern Analogy:
One Mouse with Many Genetic Fathers

Of course, a child cannot have more than one father: two men cannot contribute to the genetic inheritance of one child. The complex nature by which chromosomal characteristics can be transferred from one source to another, however, has recently been discovered. For example, one of the most powerful tools of modern genetic and molecular biological research is the ability to create a transgenic animal (usually a mouse). This is a mouse in which special carriers (such as viruses) have been used to carry genes from one species to another. For example, it is currently believed that the absence of a single protein made by one gene causes the severe respiratory disease cystic fibrosis. The gene that produces this protein recently has been isolated and transferred to a mouse where it can be more rapidly studied.

We stand at the threshhold of an era when the exact causes of some of the most dreadful pediatric diseases, such as cystic fibrosis and muscular dystrophy, are being identified and treatments involving gene therapy may be close at hand. These treatments, and this work, can only be advanced by the use of animals for research. Those who oppose the use of animal research should see for themselves what is being done in the research labs to care humanely for these animals. I cannot fathom the rationale for not progressing with research necessary to save the lives of literally thousands of children because mice must be sacrificed. [SAA]

Development of the Fetus:
Early Embryology

The Sages were fascinated by the process of pregnancy and the development of the fetus. They described the developing fetus in the following way:

It has been taught: What is the form of the human embryo?—At the beginning of its formation it is like the [species of locust called] *rashon*: Its two eyes resemble two fly-drippings, likewise its two nostrils and two ears; its two arms are like two threads of crimson silk, its mouth is like a barley-grain, its trunk like a lentil, whilst the rest of its limbs are pressed together like a formless object, and it is with regard to this that he [i.e., the Psalmist] said, "Your eyes have seen my unformed substance" (Psalm 139:16). If it be a female, it has an incision lengthwise like a barley-grain; it has no incisions indicating the outlines of hands and feet.

How does the embryo lie in its mother's womb?—It is folded up and lying like a writing-tablet. Its head lies between its knees, its two hands rest on its temples, its two heels on its two buttocks; its mouth is closed, but its navel is open; its food is that which its mother eats, its drink is that which its mother drinks, and it does not discharge excrement lest [thereby] it should kill its mother. When it issues forth into the air of the world, that which had been closed [the mouth] is opened, and that which had been open [the navel] is closed. (*Leviticus Rabbah*, *Tazria*, 14:8)

This is a fanciful, but not entirely unreasonable, description of early embryology, presumably based on the appearances of miscarried fetuses. The Sages correctly recognized that the fetus receives its nutrition from the mother and may have recognized the role the umbilical cord plays in that process.

The Sages incorrectly state that the fetal mouth is closed. Not only is the mouth open (ultrasound pictures of fetuses sucking their thumbs are commonplace), but it is absolutely crucial for development of the fetal lungs that the fetus swallow adequate amounts of amniotic fluid and have breathing movements of its lungs. Furthermore, urine is produced by the fetal kidneys during the latter stages of pregnancy and becomes a significant part of the amniotic fluid. Fetuses who have no or nonfunctioning kidneys *in utero* have a severe deficit of amniotic fluid and are born with very small lungs (pulmonary hypoplasia). This condition, called Potter's sequence, is usually fatal in the first days of life. Similarly, when a mother breaks her bag of water during the second trimester but is able to continue the pregnancy, the fetus is at a high risk for being born with pulmonary hypoplasia. The causes of these conditions are not entirely understood even at this time.

It is true that the fetus does not usually pass stool *in utero* during the pregnancy. However, stool is sometimes passed by the fetus during labor. This stool, called meconium, stains the amniotic fluid green and may be a sign of fetal distress, although it also occurs frequently during otherwise normal labor. If a large amount of meconium is swallowed by the infant during labor or delivery (meconium aspiration), it can damage the infant's lungs and is potentially fatal to the infant (rather than the mother, as suggested by the Sages). Many current obstetric and neonatal practices are designed to prevent such severe consequences from meconium aspiration. For example, if the amniotic fluid appears to have meconium in it, the obstetrician will place a tube in the baby's mouth before the rest of the body is delivered to "suck out" the meconium. The neonatologist will often be asked to make sure the infant is breathing well after the birth, and the infant may need more careful observation if meconium is found in the windpipe (trachea).

> When I was a resident in pediatrics we used to put our mouth to the tube, put the tube in the baby's windpipe, and carefully suck out the meconium. Yes, occasionally a bit of it would get in our mouth (not the sort of thing one mentioned to one's date that night). Currently, with concern about HIV infection, this is all done with mechanical suctioning devices. [SAA]

Developmental Milestones of the Fetus

The normal development of a fetus is outlined in the next section. It is framed in the context of permissible and prohibited prayers. In general, we are not permitted to pray for that which has already come to pass. For example, if we hear a scream coming from our neighborhood, we are not allowed to pray, "May it not be at my house," since this already either is, or is not, the case and cannot be changed by a prayer at that point.

> Within the first three days [after intercourse] a person should pray that the seed not putrefy; from the third to the fortieth day he should pray that the child should be male; from the fortieth day to three months he should pray that it should not be a *sandal*, from three months to six months he should pray that it should not be miscarried; from six months to nine months, he should pray for a safe delivery. (*B. Berachot* 60a)

The rules regarding these prayers reveal the times at which the Sages believed fetal developmental milestones took place. They recognized that conception occurred in the first days after sexual intercourse. The embryo has no external features allowing its sex to be identified until 8 or 9 weeks after conception, and the Sages believed that prayer might affect the gender of the infant during this period. Miscarriages are frequent during the first trimester, and the miscarried fetus's appearance might well have been described as fish-shaped.

The Sages, like ourselves, were intensely curious about the fetus. Part of developing a relationship with our children is being attuned to their every kick and flip in utero. Indeed, when I was pregnant I would put a pencil on my stomach and watch with glee as the baby's machinations would dislodge it. As the mother's stomach protrudes more and her movements slow down, and the baby's movements become more pronounced, it is as if the whole family gradually prepares for birth, the baby slowly intruding more and more visibly and tactually in our lives. [JZA]

Fetal Development: Bone Formation

Through careful observation, the Sages were able to discern characteristics of fetal development and related these developments to their religious beliefs. For example, they related the order in which a fetus developed muscle and bone to their belief in a beneficent and wise God.

> R. Abbahu said: The Holy One, blessed be He, has conferred a great boon on woman in this world, in that He does not commence the formation of the embryo with the sinews and bones, for if God did so begin, these would break through her womb and come out. (*Leviticus Rabbah, Tazria* 14:9)

R. Abbahu suggests that the skeleton is developed late in gestation. A tremendous amount of research has been done on fetal skeletal growth, and it turns out that R. Abbahu is right! Early in gestation, the fetus is composed principally (over 80 percent of fetal weight) of water. Gradually during the second and third trimesters the fraction of the fetal weight that is water decreases and the fraction that is bone increases. Although the bones are formed early in gestation, they have very little calcium, and therefore little strength, until the last 2 or 3 months of the pregnancy. Even at the time of birth, the fetal ribs are relatively bendable, allowing for easier birth.

Why does this matter? One important consequence is that premature infants born 2 to 3 months prematurely need tremendous amounts of calcium (and other minerals) to strengthen their bones. Breast milk, which is intended for term infants, has relatively little of these minerals compared to the amount received *in utero*. Although breast milk has other benefits for infants, including those born prematurely, neonatologists supplement the diet of very small premature infants who are fed breast milk with minerals to prevent them from developing rickets and fracturing their bones. In recent years, research has led to new, safe ways to determine how much fat, protein, and minerals infants have in their bodies. This information has been crucial to our understanding of the nutritional needs of both premature and term infants. Remarkably, despite our best efforts, it is still impossible to feed a very small premature infant so that she will have the size and body composition she would have had if she remained inside her mother throughout the third trimester.

I find that many parents have trouble understanding why it is sometimes so difficult to get small premature babies to grow at a rate comparable to what they would inside the womb. To appreciate the problems involved in feeding premature infants, remember that before birth all the nutrients go directly from placenta to baby, the gut isn't involved in selectively absorbing things (e.g., at best about half the calcium in infant formula is absorbed by a baby). Furthermore, inside the womb the baby isn't using energy to breathe, stay warm, or cry over the blood tests to which she's subjected. Finally, the preemie's stomach is very small. A 1.5-pound baby may be able to tolerate only 2 or 3 ounces of milk per day. [SAA]

Causes of Birth Defects:
Inappropriate Behavior

The causes of birth defects and illnesses quite naturally occupied the Sages, particularly because they linked the occurrence of birth defects to indecorous sexual behavior. (Incidentally, this outlook was widely held in the ancient world: Greek, Roman, and Christian authorities of this and earlier ages believed that there was a connection between proper decorum during sexual intercourse and positive outcomes for the fetus.)

> Rabbi Yohanan ben Dahavai said: The Ministering Angels told me four things: People are born lame because [their parents] overturned their table [i.e., practiced unnatural cohabitation]; mute, because they kiss "that place"; deaf, because they converse during cohabitation; blind, because they look at "that place". . . . Rabbi Yohanan said: The above is the view of Rabbi Yohanan ben Dahavai [only]. The Sages said: Jewish law is not as Rabbi Yohanan ben Dahavai, but a man may do whatever he pleases with his wife [during intercourse]. It can be compared to meat which comes from the butcher shop. If he wished to eat it salted, he eats it so; roasted, he eats it so; cooked, he eats it so; seethed, he eats it so. (B. Nedarim 20a–b)

The Sages could not mandate the limited forms of sexual behavior that they deemed proper. This is the meaning of their parable about the meat. (Women are often likened to food in rabbinic culture, and in modern culture, as well.) Just as meat, as long as it is kosher, may be eaten any way one wishes once it is taken home, so a man, once married, may have sexual intercourse with his wife in any way that he desires. (Of course, we would hope that a more enlightened, egalitarian approach to marital relations exists today and that one partner is not viewed as a consumable object, while the other partner is the "consumer.") Rabbi Yohanan ben Dahavai could not legislate his desire for decorous sexual behavior; he could only make it the ideal and suggest that serious penalties would adhere to those forms of sexual contact that he deemed less desirable but nonetheless legal. We note, however, that Rabbi Yohanan ben Dahavai's is only an individual's opinion and is not adopted as Jewish law.

The Sages did, however, associate the spirit with which sexual intercourse was performed with the emotional temperament of the child it produced.

> Whoever compels his wife to the [marital] obligation will have unworthy children. . . . Each woman who solicits her husband to the [marital] obligation will have children the like of whom did not exist even in the generation of Moses. (B. Eruvin 100b)

We note that the Sages apparently did not approve of marital rape and associated it with unworthy children. Conversely, if a woman actively sought sexual relations with her husband, it was thought that children from such a union would be meritorious.

In addition, the Sages associated birth defects and disease in the newborn with failure to observe the laws of niddah.

> Who causes a newborn child to be leprous?—Its mother, who did not observe her period of separation (niddah). . . . Each man who goes unto his wife while she is a

niddah makes his children leprous . . . and these [the children] apply to their parents the following verse, "Our fathers have sinned, and are not; and we have borne their sins" (Lamentations 5:7). (*Leviticus Rabbah, Tazria* 15:5)

Parents are strongly urged, through this teaching, to control their desire for sexual intercourse during the period of *niddah*, under the threat of conceiving children who will be born leprous.

The Sages, then, saw sexual intercourse and any conception issuing from it as part of a larger network of values. Sex is not simply a physical act for the Sages. It is part of an interlocking network of *mitzvot* that, if engaged in properly, will bring great rewards to the participants. And if it is engaged in with a sense of violence or compulsion it will bring hardship to the participants through the ensuing conception and birth of a child forever characterized by the act of its conception.

The Sages, like almost everyone who faces suffering and tragedy, sought to find meaning in that suffering. The obvious lesson they drew from the suffering of children born with birth defects, and the suffering of their parents, was that pain should lead to a greater observance of the mitzvot. *The Sages saw the* mitzvot *as a way of saying, in effect, "We are in a partnership with God. God demands certain things from us and there are things we do not understand about life and its processes. That given, we can follow these guidelines that tradition tells us give meaning and order to life when life feels chaotic and meaningless, as it does when we face great tragedies." [JZA, SAA]*

Birth Defects:
Guilty Feelings of the Parents

These passages suggest that parents may be at fault for the birth of children with congenital malformations or serious illnesses. This is a concept that has survived the ages intact and, if anything, has become more common. Although the absence of any medical understanding of these conditions in ancient days naturally led the Sages to believe in supernatural and "moral" causes for birth defects, we must use our current knowledge to rethink this paradigm and the implications of it.

Although occasionally some parental fault may be involved (as in drug-addicted newborns), rarely is a newborn's malformation or illness directly related to anything its parents have done wrong. Yet the sense of guilt and of parental (usually maternal) responsibility is overwhelming in such situations. Numerous popular articles incorrectly imply that if a pregnant woman takes a pain pill or has an alcoholic drink she will irreparably damage her fetus. Our society increasingly believes that whenever something goes wrong with a baby, someone must be blamed.

Neonatologists face this issue regularly. I remember a baby boy born with severe congenital malformations while I was on call one night. At that time I was still training to be a neonatologist and was stunned to hear the mother ask me if her son's problems were her fault. It had never occurred to me (then an unmarried, childless pediatrician) that anyone could blame a mother for something like that. The mother proceeded to tell me that her mother-in-law had called and blamed her for producing a deformed baby.

Since then, I've learned that blame, external or self-inflicted, is common in this situation and is difficult to deal with and overcome. Significant marital strife and personal agony can result from such misplaced guilt. Whether they specifically ask or not, I frequently tell parents, "this was not your fault." [SAA]

Because blame isn't to be assigned doesn't imply that it isn't important to learn all we can about why a malformation or illness occurred. Genetic counseling may be appropriate regarding future pregnancies. Even if no more children are planned many parents wish to understand as fully as possible what happened to their infant.

One difficult challenge for a Jewish neonatologist is considering how to counsel families regarding autopsies. Traditional Jewish views strongly discourage them unless absolutely necessary. However, few of my families are Jewish and I keep this perspective out of it. One solution would be to tell parents, "It's up to you" and whereas ultimately that's true, it avoids the question that really interests them, which is, "What would we learn from an autopsy?" In most cases I tend not to push very hard, especially in the case of extremely premature infants where it is relatively unlikely (but not inconceivable) that the autopsy will show things not already apparent about what happened. In some cases, such as when there is a congenital defect, I push very hard for an autopsy. Appropriate genetic counseling depends on learning exactly what the problem was, and there remains no substitute to an autopsy for fully identifying most congenital defects. [SAA]

Another source of confusion is the very common misconception that prenatal testing will ensure a healthy, "nondeformed" baby. This is not even close to the truth. Mothers will say, "Why did my baby have a malformed heart (or a severe infection, etc.) even though I took care of myself and had an ultrasound and/or amniocentesis? How could this have been missed?" Prenatal testing takes various forms, including blood tests (i.e., alpha fetoprotein measurement), to screen for the possibility of spina bifida, ultrasounds that identify some fetal structural or growth abnormalities, and amniocentesis, from which one obtains, among other things, genetic chromosome analysis. Each of these tests can identify some, but not all, problems with the developing fetus. There is no guarantee of a healthy baby despite every known form of prenatal care and testing. Adequate prenatal care can lessen the risk of problems, but no degree of care or testing can guarantee a "perfect" baby.

> It seems to me that the complexity of prenatal diagnostic issues facing parents has reached a level far beyond what many families can hope to understand or make decisions about. This situation will only worsen as more diagnostic tests are developed. This doesn't mean that they shouldn't be developed. However, I readily confess that there are already numerous conditions that can be identified prenatally that would cause me great ambivalence if they were identified prenatally in my child.
>
> In any case, the array of decisions and tests are already numbing. For example, a common scenario is for a mother to have a "routine" blood test at about 18 weeks gestation called an alpha-fetoprotein measurement. If this test gives an abnormally high result, she may be advised to have an amniocentesis to further identify whether a spinal cord defect or other

neourological problem might be present. However, the amniocentisis itself carries a risk of miscarriage (about 1 in 200 or less when done with direct ultrasonographic guidance) and many spinal defects can be identified by ultrasound. All these choices—and we haven't even gotten to the issue of what to do if the amnio/ultrasound are abnormal. [SAA]

Prenatal Influences

Prenatal influences are not limited to the mode of conception alone. A mother's nutrition and contact with deleterious and beneficial influences were deemed to affect the fetus.

1. A woman who couples in a mill will have epileptic children.
2. One who couples on the ground will have children with long necks.
3. [A woman] who treads on the blood of an ass will have scabby bald children.
4. One who eats mustard will have intemperate children.
5. One who eats cress will have bleary-eyed children.
6. One who eats fish brine will have children with blinking eyes.
7. One who eats clay will have ugly children.
8. One who drinks intoxicating liquor will have black children.
9. One who eats meat and drinks wine will have children of a robust constitution.
10. One who eats eggs will have children with big eyes.
11. One who eats fish will have graceful children.
12. One who eats parsley (*karpasa*) will have beautiful children.

13. One who eats coriander will have stout children.
14. One who eats *etrog* will have fragrant children. The daughter of King Shapur, whose mother had eaten *etrog* [while she was pregnant] with her, used to be presented before her father as his principal perfume. (*B. Ketubot* 60b–61a)

Perhaps the Sages who developed these concepts observed women who, for example, ate mustard and then had hot-headed children. Or perhaps they noted hot-tempered children and wondered why they had such temperaments and attributed it to their mothers' consumption of hot foods while pregnant.

> *If you are lucky enough to be pregnant during Sukkot, then you can take the* etrog *(a citron) and use the zest or the fruit for marmalade or other cooking to keep this tradition alive.* [SAA, JZA]

The latter statements in this passage suggest ways that parents can improve their unborn offspring. Most of these are associative, that is, fish swim gracefully, egg yolks resemble large eyes. Among the negative admonitions, of note is the distinction between numbers 8 and 9: drinking wine is permissible, but intoxication is not. Fetal alcohol syndrome, associated with maternal consumption of large amounts of alcohol, especially in early pregnancy, has a number of negative effects, including abnormalities in facial appearance and motor coordination, as well as retardation. It is possible that this passage refers to this syndrome, although it may merely relate to the appearance of intoxication in adults.

It is easy to understand why the passages relating sexual "misconduct" to birth defects were included in rabbinic literature: they relate standards for sexual behavior to birth outcomes. However, this passage has no moral overtones to it at all, yet it is included in rabbinic literature. The Sages, particularly the Sages of Babylonia, learned what they could from folk medicine, especially when it related to legal issues, and considered this holy knowledge. They tried to incorporate as many spheres of knowledge into their thinking as possible.

Protecting the Fetus against Premature Delivery

The Sages were filled with wonder at the process of pregnancy and birth. One of the most praiseworthy parts of the process, in their eyes, was that the fetus stayed in the womb. They noted that animals walk horizontally and believed gravity helped keep the fetus inside the animals. The Sages attributed the miracle of a closed womb in women, who walk upright, to God's beneficence:

> In the [usual] way of the world, if a person holds a bag of coins with its opening [pointed] downward, do not the coins scatter? Now the fetus has its abode in the mother's womb [whose opening is pointed downward], but the Holy One, blessed be He, guards it that it shall not fall out and die. (*Leviticus Rabbah* 14:3)

The amniotic sac (membrane) and the tightly closed cervix of the uterus protect the human fetus from premature delivery. Rupture of the membranes before the infant has reached full term is a common problem and leads to a significant number of premature births. Premature rup-

ture of the membranes has many causes, including infection and trauma. In many cases, even after premature
rupture of the membrane, delivery can be postponed for
several days to several weeks, allowing the fetus to grow
and develop.

Premature Birth: 7- and 8-Month Fetuses

The Sages believed that there were two sorts of viable
fetuses: those born after 7 months of gestation and those
born after 9 months. However, infants born at 8 months
gestation age were not deemed viable. Current concepts
about the premature birth of infants are quite different
from those the Sages held. In particular, we no longer
believe that there are two sorts of healthy births, at 7 and
9 months. The Sages strongly held this belief as we can
see from the following passage:

> On account of an infant born at seven [months of gesta-
> tion] they override [the prohibitions] of the Sabbath. On
> account of an infant born at eight [months], they do not
> override [the prohibitions of] the Sabbath. [If] it is a mat-
> ter of doubt whether it is born at seven [months of preg-
> nancy] or eight, they do not override [the restrictions of]
> the Sabbath on his account. An infant born after eight
> [months of pregnancy], lo, it is tantamount to a stone.
> And it is forbidden to move it about. However, his mother
> bends over him and nurses him. (*T. Shabbat* 15:5)

Here we see quite clearly that a baby born at 8 months of
gestational age was viewed as not viable, while babies
born at 7 and 9 months of gestational age were considered viable in every respect; therefore, the Sabbath could

be violated on their account. (We note that this does not reflect modern Jewish law.)

Another passage confirms that this was a widely held belief in the Sages' day and links it to a text from the Torah.

> "Unto the woman He said, I will greatly multiply (harbah arbeh) the pain of your childbearing; in sorrow shall you bring forth children" (Genesis 3:16). R. Abba bar Zutra said in R. Samuel's name: Every [fetus] that has [developed to the numerical value of] harbah, I will multiply (arbeh): i.e., a fetus that has developed for two hundred and twelve days is viable. R. Huna said: When the fetus is so formed as to be born at nine [months], and it is born either at seven [months] or at eight [months], it is not viable. When it is formed so as to be born at seven [months], but is actually born at eight [months], it is viable, and all the more so if it is born at nine [months]. . . . R. Berekhiah in R. Samuel's name said: A woman can give birth only at 271, 272 or 273 [days], which is at nine [months] plus the days of conception. [The Sages believed a woman could conceive within three days of intercourse.]
>
> "Your pain" refers to the suffering of conception; "your travail" to the suffering of pregnancy; "in pain," to the suffering of miscarriages; "shall you bring forth" to the suffering of childbirth; "children" to the suffering involved in the upbringing of children. (Genesis Rabbah 20:6)

This passage, from the Midrash collection Genesis Rabbah, reiterates the viewpoint that a "7-month baby" can live if born at 7, 8, or 9 months, while a "9-month baby" can live only if born at 9 months. The Sages play on a special verb form in Genesis 3:16 that involves a doubling of the words' core idea and indicates intensity. So, here, the double form *harbah arbeh* means literally, "multiplying I will multiply"; that is, "I will multiply a great deal." However, the Sages often endow each part of this double verb form with its own meaning.

They also use gymmatria, the practice of attributing numerical values to words that suggest hidden meanings in the text. The word *harbah*, part of the phrase "I will greatly multiply," has the following numerical value:

```
hey   =    5
reish = 200
bet   =    2
hey   =    5
           212
```

The Sages therefore take the passage to mean that God will multiply (*arbeh*, the other half of the verb form) those babies who are mature at 212 days, or 7 months. The Sages see here a hint at the concept of 7- and 9-month babies.

Finally, they finish their explication of Genesis 3:16 by noting that God could simply have said, "I will make childbirth hurt," rather than the sentence as we have it. Whenever there is an apparently needless repetition in the Torah text, the Sages ferret out the hidden meaning behind the words, for they assumed that there were no superfluous words in Torah. Therefore, they take the apparently superfluous words in this sentence to refer to different parts of the process of conceiving, carrying, bearing, and caring for children, all of which involve some suffering.

This whole passage may have been difficult to understand. In the Jewish tradition, texts are understood on four levels: (1) the simple, plain level, (2) a level that is hinted at, (3) a level that applies to Jewish law and lore, and (4) a deep mystical level. This method of using numerology is an example of level 2, finding meanings only hinted at in the text. Some people absolutely love this method, others think it's silly. If it speaks to you, that's wonderful. If it doesn't, don't worry. You still have three other methods to choose from. [JZA]

Premature Infants:
The Historical Context of Rabbinic Views

Before considering modern issues of prematurity and viability it is important to put these writings into a historical context. The belief that healthy babies were only delivered after 7 or 9 months of pregnancy was widespread in the ancient world, as can be seen from the writings of contemporary medical authorities. For example, Hippocrates believed that a person's life was arranged in periods of 7: the embryo acquired all its essential parts in 7 days. Likewise a viable baby could be born at 7 months gestational age, while an 8-month baby could not survive. The ancient physician Soranus likewise believed that there were two types of healthy births: at 7 and 9 months.

It is interesting to speculate on what the Sages and the other ancient sources might have been thinking of when they describe healthy "7-month" babies. At 31 weeks (7 months), most premature infants will have difficulty adequately nursing. Currently, we would routinely provide intravenous fluid followed by feedings via a tube into the infant's stomach until the infant was able to nurse or bottle feed. Usually it isn't until about 33 or 34 weeks that most premature infants learn to coordinate their sucking, swallowing, and breathing and are able to nurse (or bottle feed) adequately. With effort and careful attention to keeping the infant warm, however, it is likely that some 31-week infants would have survived in ancient days without any intervention.

An additional possibility is that the healthy "7-month" babies the Sages describe might have included some low birth weight babies born after 9 months (today, such babies are referred to as being "light for dates" or "small for gestational age"). This is a relatively common situation and can be associated with many conditions, such as maternal high blood pressure during pregnancy. Such infants, even if quite small, might have been expected to do well. Perhaps the most likely explanation is that the Sages were occasionally uncertain of when a woman became pregnant and adopted the prevailing Greek opinion that full-size babies could occur after 7 or 9 months of pregnancy. This view is supported by the following passage:

> It is easy to understand why [a divorcee or widow] shall not marry after waiting a period of just two months since that would create a doubt as to whether the child is a nine-month one of the first [husband] or a seven-month one of the second [husband]. Rather, let her wait one month [only] and then marry, so that, should she give birth at seven months, the child would be a seven-month one of the second [husband] and should she give birth at eight months the child would obviously be a nine-month one of the first [husband]. (B. Yebamot 42a)

The need to time the second marriage to be sure who the father was strongly suggests that the Sages believed that after 7 months a full-size baby might be born (conceived from her new husband) who would be indistinguishable from a 9-month baby (conceived from her first husband).

These beliefs persisted for centuries. In eighteenth-century England, labor was sometimes induced during the seventh month to avoid a difficult labor at full term. It was not until this century that the doctrine that the "7-month infant lived and the 8-month infant died" was recognized as a superstition. One potential explanation for the lingering of this belief into the nineteenth and twentieth centuries is the suggestion that 7-month babies were given special care while 8-month babies were treated in the same way as those born at term. Of course, like other folk beliefs, this one has not entirely disappeared, as evidenced by this recent review of ancient obstetrical practice: "Interestingly, the opinion that birth in the eighth month is even more dangerous than in the seventh month has remained a popular folk belief to this day. In fact, it may often be found even among midwives and hospital nurses who are unaware of this belief's ancient and medieval origins."[3]

What a remarkable history this concept has had! It began with Hippocrates (or earlier) and survived at least into the eighteenth century as a medical concept and into the twentieth century as a folk belief. Even the author of a pediatric textbook of the 1920s felt this concept important enough to need specific refutation.[4]

In case there is any doubt, rest assured that, assuming the pregnancy is progressing normally, it is much better to be born at 8 months than at 7 months gestation. However, modern neonatologists are quite familiar with large "8-month babies" who have severe immaturity of the lungs (hyaline membrane disease) and can be extremely ill. With modern therapy these infants virtually always survive. Currently, survival of infants born at 8 months is comparable to that of full-term infants.

> *The problem of 8-month babies with lung immaturity is much more common for boys than girls. It appears that boys may not always produce the chemical that is necessary for the lungs to expand properly as early in gestation as girls. We used to see this commonly with scheduled cesarean sections for a woman who had had a previous C-section. Unfortunately, if the dating of the pregnancy was off a bit, we would end up with a very slightly premature, but very sick, little boy.* [SAA]

Childbirth

The process of childbirth is important and exhilarating—and painful! The Sages considered this process of transition from fetus to independent child to be risky for the mother, and indeed, maternal death during childbirth was certainly more common then than in our own day. Currently maternal mortality is approximately 1 in 50,000 pregnancies and has decreased over a hundredfold in the past 70 years alone.

Because of the need for basic care for the mother and infant, the Sages ruled that the needs of a woman in labor and of her newborn child override the restrictions of the Sabbath:

> They may deliver a woman on the Sabbath and summon for her a midwife from any place whatever, and they may profane the Sabbath for her sake and tie up the umbilical

cord. Rabbi Yose says, They may even cut it. (*M. Shabbat* 18:3)

What is the basic care that a mother and infant require? They need someone to aid in the birth process, and that person is not restricted by Sabbath laws in caring for them. For example, prohibitions against kindling a fire, cutting, tearing, or writing are not enforced while helping a woman through the birth process.

In its commentary on this mishnah, the Bavli attempts to define what sort of labor is advanced enough that one may desecrate the Sabbath on the "laborer's" behalf.

> Rav Judah said in Samuel's name: If a woman is in confinement, as long as the uterus is open, whether she said, "I need it" or she did not say, "I need it," we desecrate the Sabbath on her account. If the uterus is closed, whether she says, "I need it" or she does not say, "I need it," we may not desecrate the Sabbath for her; that is how Rav Ashi recited it.
>
> Mar Zutra recited it thus: Rav Judah said in Samuel's name: If a woman is in confinement, as long as the uterus is open, whether she says, "I need it" or she says, "I do not need it," we desecrate the Sabbath for her. If the uterus is closed, if she says, "I need it," we desecrate the Sabbath for her; if she does not say, "I need it," we do not desecrate the Sabbath for her.
>
> Ravina asked Meremar: Mar Zutra recited it in the direction of leniency [while] Rav Ashi recited it in the direction of stringency; which is the law?—The law is as Mar Zutra, replied he: where [a matter of] life is in doubt we are lenient.
>
> From when is the opening of the uterus? Abaye said: From when she sits on the seat of travail. Rav Huna son

of Rav Joshua said: From when the blood slowly flows down; and others say, From when her friends carry her by her arms.

For how long is the opening of the uterus: Abaye said: Three days. Rava said in Rav Judah's name: Seven. Others say: Thirty. (B. Shabbat 128b–129a)

The Sages differed in their definition of what constituted labor advanced enough to justify desecrating the Sabbath. Rav Ashi is more strict and implies that the woman must be in labor with dilation of her cervix for the Sabbath to be violated on her behalf. Mar Zutra, on the other hand, is more lenient and did not require any evidence of cervical dilation. In deciding the halakhah, Jewish law, the more lenient opinion is accepted since a matter of life and death is involved.

The question of when labor has begun and ended also had to be decided. The differences of opinion probably related to differences in perception regarding early labor and "false" labor. Those opting for a longer time (30 days) almost surely were recognizing the difficulty of the last month of pregnancy and the needs of a mother for additional comforts then, the providing of which might violate the Sabbath. This is consistent with another passage in which the Sages ask:

> "How long is hard labor?" Rabbi Meir says, "Even forty or fifty days." Rabbi Judah says, "Sufficient for her is her [ninth] month." Rabbi Yose and Rabbi Shimon say, "Hard labor continues no longer than two weeks." (M. Niddah 4:5)

Regardless of when one considers that labor has begun, necessary care for a woman in labor must be given.

The Sages were quite aware that, as hard labor pro-
gressed, a woman's life might be endangered by the failure of the baby to emerge, for example, because of a trans-
verse position. In such a case, the Mishnah allows the child
to be sacrificed to save the mother's life.

> If a woman is in hard labor, the child in her womb may
> be cut up and brought out member by member, because
> [her] life has priority over the child's life. But if the greater
> part of the child has emerged, it may not be touched, since
> one life may not be sacrificed [to preserve] another. (M.
> Oholot 7:6)

Until the infant emerges from the woman's body it is considered to be merely a part of her that might kill her, and
so it may be sacrificed. Similarly, the Sages would have
no hesitation in recommending that a gangrenous foot
be amputated to save a person's life. However, once the
infant has partially emerged, it is considered to be a person whose life may not be sacrificed for the mother's. This
is a key passage in defining the Sages' attitude toward
abortion, an issue we will examine more fully in Chapter
Nine.

> This belief that the baby hasn't arrived until it is actu-
> ally born and living is reflected in the Jewish custom
> of avoiding having baby furniture or clothing deliv-
> ered until the baby is born. [JZA, SAA]

Birth Lore: Boys versus Girls

A great deal of folk medicine regarding the differences
between pregnancy with a boy and one with a girl is, to

this day, widely circulated. The Sages also believed that pregnancy and delivery with male and female infants differed.

> Our Rabbis taught: During the first three months the embryo occupies the lowest chamber, during the middle ones it occupies the middle chamber and during the last months it occupies the uppermost chamber; and when its time to emerge arrives it turns over and then emerges, and this is the cause of the woman's pains. This also agrees with what was taught: The pains of a female birth are more intense than those of a male birth. . . . Why are the pains of a female birth greater than those of a male birth? The female emerges in the position she assumes during intercourse and the male emerges in the position he assumes during intercourse. (B. Niddah 31a)

This can be compared to the similar belief held by the Greeks and later medieval writers:

> The belief of the ancient Greek philosophers in the natural superiority of the male, the "perfect being" over the female, was accepted almost unquestionably by medieval writers. . . . This belief is reflected in [the medieval] manuscript which states that "the male emerges with less anguish than the female," a statement having absolutely no corroboration in modern science.[5]

We note that the Sages' description of which chamber a fetus occupies follows the appearance of the mother's belly as the pregnancy progresses. The pregnancy does, indeed, first make itself evident low in the abdomen and gradually expands upward. However, their description of the turning of males and females is not consistent with medical knowledge today. Most infants emerge with their faces downward. Medically this is referred to as occiput anterior and is associated with an easier labor and delivery than a baby born facing upwards (occiput posterior). The Sages' comments reflect their knowledge of this fact, but they incorrectly relate the gender of the child to its birth position.

Pain and Childbirth

The process of childbirth, thankfully, need no longer be as painful as it was in ages past. Modern anesthetics allow for significant pain relief during labor. However, women in the Sages' days had no such aid and obviously suffered more in the process of bringing children into the world. Anyone who has been through labor will probably recognize the plausibility of the following scenario outlined by R. Shimon ben Yohai.

> R. Shimon ben Yohai was asked by his disciples: Why did the Torah ordain that a woman after childbirth should bring a sacrifice? He replied: When she kneels in bearing she swears impetuously that she will have no intercourse with her husband. The Torah therefore ordained that she should bring a sacrifice. (B. Niddah 31b)

I must confess that, before my first child was born, I thought this was simply an unenlightened male view of childbirth. However, having now been through the process, I find this scenario quite easy to believe. [JZA]

Keeping one's perspective during labor is dificult. In fact, a term used in rabbinic literature to describe a person who is intermittently insane is related to the term used to describe the pangs of childbirth (safah/nistafah). The remarkable process whereby one is almost irrational with pain and then of (relatively) normal mind within a minute may indeed lead to impetuous statements that should not be taken too seriously by fathers or other innocent bystanders. Fortunately for fathers, mothers tend to forget some of the less pleasant aspects of labor.

Controversy exists over the appropriate use of pain relief measures, such as intravenous narcotics and epidural anesthesia, during labor. Opponents of the use of these medications express concern that these medications are inappropriate for laboring mothers and may be unsafe for mother or infant. Because of this viewpoint, achieving an unmedicated labor and delivery has become an important goal for many women. Certainly, women who opt for "natural childbirth" should be supported.

We should, however, take a balanced approach toward pain relief during delivery. Pressuring women to forgo pain relief during labor is as inappropriate as its injudicious use.

In general, women should be free to make whatever decision they choose (in consultation with their obstetrical caregivers) in this matter without undue coercion in any direction. I do not believe, however, that the appropriate use of anesthetic techniques during labor is harmful to the infant and reject the notion that mothers are subjecting their children to unnecessary risk by receiving pain relief. [SAA]

Concluding Thoughts
on Conception and Pregnancy

Significant advances have been made by medical scientists in our understanding of conception, fetal development, and childbirth. And yet so much remains unchanged: parents still ponder God's role in this process; they still feel guilt and dismay when a pregnancy fails or a baby is born ill; mothers may still suffer pain in the process of childbirth. The Sages' insights sometimes agree with modern medical opinions and sometimes our modern view of medicine causes us to reconsider not just the obvious medical issues, but our underlying assumptions about parental responsibilities and needs.

5

The Newborn Infant

A newborn's first moments of life outside the womb and his first contact with his parents are moments of wonder, but also moments of evaluation. Although we may already have counted our child's fingers and toes via ultrasound, we are clearly able to see more of the child once he has emerged as an independent entity. Now, as in ancient days, parents are relieved to hear their newborn's first cry.

Newborns are so small, so vulnerable, so warm, and so beautiful that they call forth a deep response in us. Holding them, feeding them, and comforting them seems the most natural, comfortable thing to do. This phase passes with lightning speed (although it may not seem that way during the first month or so of sleepless nights). All too soon, they are crawling and toddling away from us under their own power. Never again do they allow us to hold them and rock them as much as they do at this stage. The message? Enjoy it while you can because it is gone before you know it.

> *On the other hand, a friend once said wisely, look-*
> *ing at her sleeping infant, "You know, I often wish he*
> *was asleep when he's awake, but I rarely wish he was*
> *awake while he's asleep."* [SAA, JZA]

Care of the Newborn Infant:
Salting and Swaddling

The Prophet Ezekiel, who prophesied in Babylonia between 593 and 571 B.C.E., provides us with some of our
earliest information about the procedures used to care for
infants at their birth in ancient days:

> And as for your nativity, in the day you were born your
> navel was not cut, neither were you washed in water for
> cleansing; you were not salted at all, nor swaddled at all.
> No eye pitied you, to do any of these unto you, to have
> compassion upon you; but you were cast out in the open
> field in the loathsomeness of your person, in the day that
> you were born. (Ezekiel 16:4–5)

This passage is part of a rebuke to Jerusalem in which
the city is personified, in part, as an abandoned infant.
The prophet therefore uses social norms, easily understood by his listeners, to describe this infant's/city's plight.
From this we can gather that the normal care of a newborn involved cutting the umbilical cord, washing the infant, salting it, and swaddling it. These, it would seem, were
the minimum requirements for newborn care in Ezekiel's
day. The Sages used these verses as a basis for describing what actions could be taken for a baby even if they
violated the Sabbath (*B. Shabbat* 129b). That is, the
practices which were mentioned by Ezekiel continued to

be considered absolutely essential for the health and well-being of a baby in the Sages' day, 800 to 1,100 years later.

The most unusual of these treatments from our current perspective would be the salting of a newborn. This custom was apparently borrowed from the Greeks and was thought to lead to a thicker skin, perhaps less prone to rashes or infections. Apparently the salt used was a form of bicarbonate and probably served as a soap for the newborn. Salting was advocated by Soranus and by Galen (130–200 c.e.) and mentioned in medical textbooks at least into the sixteenth century. This custom was practiced in the Near East at least into the early part of the twentieth century, based on traditional beliefs that salting strengthened the skin and even improved the child's character.

The swaddling referred to is not just bundling the infant in a blanket as is currently done. Rather, it referred to a very constrictive, almost mummifying, wrapping that was believed to help straighten the limbs. We now recognize that this is not a useful practice and that the apparent bowing of the newborns limbs will usually naturally straighten as the infant matures. Tight constriction in a blanket may be dangerous because of the limitation it places on the child's ability to turn and move from a position that may be suffocating. The practice of swaddling was advocated in ancient days by Soranus and continued to be practiced into the early twentieth century in some areas.

It's important to keep in mind that sage pediatric advice can change. For many years, it was taught that infants should be placed on their stomachs to lessen the risks of refluxing food from the stomach to the windpipe. Recently, however, several studies have suggested that there is an increased risk of crib death (SIDS—sudden infant death syndrome) in infants who are placed on their stomachs, as they may become smothered in the bedding or blankets. Placing infants on their back or on their side (unless they have evidence of reflux) is now strongly recommended. This certainly will not solve the problem of SIDS, but some studies suggest it will decrease its incidence substantially.

It remains a bit of an art to bundle a newborn in hospital blankets. When I teach medical students how to perform physical examinations on newborns I always have them change a diaper and rebundle the babies after the examination. Usually, the nurses have to restrain themselves from laughing too much as they watch the medical students try to figure out how to do these tasks. [SAA]

"Mother's" Teachings
on Newborn Resuscitation

As we have already mentioned, Abaye's "mother" is often cited in the Bavli as a source of medical knowledge. For example, we have this collection of her teachings regarding the care of newborn infants.

And Abaye said: Mother told me, If an infant cannot suck, his lips are cold. What is the remedy? A vessel of burning coals should be brought and held near his nostrils, so as to heat it, then he will suck.

And Abaye said: Mother told me, If an infant does not breathe, he should be fanned with a fan and he will breathe.

And Abaye said: Mother told me, If an infant cannot breathe easily, his mother's after-birth should be brought and rubbed over him, [and] he will breathe easily.

And Abaye said: Mother told me, If an infant is too thin, his mother's after-birth should be brought and rubbed over him from its narrow end to its wide end; if he is too fat [it should be rubbed] from the wide to the narrow end. (B. Shabbat 134a)

This is truly a remarkable passage. Abaye's mother was clearly versed in midwifery and the care of newborns. Even in ancient days, those who cared for infants created a categorization, or diagnostic, scheme to deal with newborns and developed standard modes of treatment for various conditions. There would appear to be nothing specifically Jewish about this passage, except that it is included in the Talmud and cited in the name of one of our greatest Sages. Yet this is a religious matter. Life is precious. Preserving it is a religious duty and the Sages, through their connection with tradition, were thought to be the conduits of the knowledge that could help people fulfill this obligation.

The teachings Abaye quotes demonstrate the ideas held in that era regarding newborn resuscitation. In dealing with the infant who does not breathe, it was suggested that he be fanned and if necessary rubbed with his own placenta. One can surmise that this constituted an attempt to stimulate the infant and perhaps to dry the infant (by fanning). We continue to recognize the importance of drying the newborn, and this is done rapidly after birth. It was not always the custom to sever the umbilical cord in the first minutes of life (some Sages did not advocate cutting the umbilical cord on the Sabbath, although the cutting was deemed permissible). Rubbing the baby with the placenta may therefore have been a way of transferring additional blood to the fetus. For an infant who would not nurse, it was suggested his mouth be warmed.

Current Ideas Regarding Newborn Resuscitation

To understand how newborn resuscitation has advanced since the time of the Sages, we must begin with a bit of background as to what happens to the fetal heart and lungs at birth. Prior to birth, oxygenated blood from mother via the placenta enters the fetal veins and flows into the right side of the heart. Because the fetal lungs do not supply oxygen, the fetus has a passageway inside the heart (foramen ovale) and a vessel outside the heart (ductus arteriosis) by which this oxygenated placental blood bypasses the nonfunctioning fetal lungs and goes directly toward supplying the body's need for oxygen.

At birth, with the very rapid cutoff of oxygen from the mother, the infant's circulation must change rapidly. Not only must the infant now breathe so blood can be oxygenated in the lungs, but the blood must quickly start flowing through the lungs instead of bypassing them. This change does not occur instantly. The change to a postnatal circulation takes at least several hours in term infants and frequently even longer in premature infants. These first hours are unquestionably the most critical period of an infant's life and are the period in which intervention may be necessary to assist a newborn whose circulation has not made this transition.

Decades of research and clinical experience have led to highly sophisticated methods for assessing and caring for infants during this crucial transition period. Although we recognize the critical importance of basic needs such as warmth and dryness for stimulating the infant to breathe we have huge advantages now that the ancients did not have. We can help the infant by clearing his airway (suction), by giving oxygen, or in severe situations, by breathing for the infant using oxygen delivered by a "bag and mask" or by a machine (mechanical ventilation).

This is an area of tremendous ongoing interest and research, as the inability to successfully make the transition from fetal to infant circulation remains one of the most common causes of severe illness in newborns. For example, infants who swallow large amounts of their stool during labor or who lacked adequate oxygen during labor are at risk of having their circulation remain as it was *in utero* (persistent fetal circulation, also called persistent pulmonary hypertension). In this case, blood continues to bypass the lungs, but, of course, there is no oxygenated blood coming from mother for the baby. Frequently this condition responds to routine medical treatment, such as providing oxygen or mechanical ventilation. Failure of the infant to respond to such therapy in the past, however, led to a high risk of death in the first days of life. Two of the newest methods for treating this condition are (1) placing the infant on cardiopulmonary bypass therapy for a few days until the circulation is able to "fix itself" (ECMO—extracorporeal membrane oxygenation) and (2) giving infants small amounts of nitric oxide.

ECMO represents one of the most novel and contro-versial developments in medicine over the past de-

cade. Remarkably, the technology exists to place a baby as small as 4.5 pounds on bypass so that the heart and lungs can be nearly completely supported. As one might expect this has risks, such as bleeding or permanent damage to important blood vessels associated with it, but the development of ECMO has unquestionably saved the lives of many babies. The trick is to decide when a baby's risk of dying is greater than the risks associated with the use of ECMO. Not surprisingly, it has been very difficult to perform research studies of this topic.

Neonatologists have long sought a magic potion that would "mature" the circulation without harming the infant. We keep getting closer (with nitric oxide, for instance), but no such potion has yet been proven to exist. [SAA]

Currently neonatologists don't use fans or the placenta to stimulate the infant. Instead, we gently rub the infant's back or stimulate his feet. We also do not spank the infant to stimulate him.

We don't believe in spanking children, in the delivery room or in second grade, but more on that later (see Chapter Eight). [JZA, SAA]

Circumcision: An Ancient Ritual

The birth of a Jewish boy means that the parents, in addition to coping with life with a newborn, must begin planning the joyous celebration that accompanies the performance of one of the most central *mitzvot* in Judaism: *brit milah*, the covenant of circumcision.

The origins of this covenant are as old as Judaism itself, stretching back to the time of Abraham, the first Jew,
whom God commanded:

> And you shall be circumcised in the flesh of your fore-
> skin; and it shall be a token of a covenant between Me
> and you. And he that is eight days old shall be circum-
> cised among you, every male throughout your genera-
> tions, he that is born in the house, or bought with money
> of any foreigner, that is not of your seed. (Genesis 17: 11–
> 12)

The act of circumcision, to be considered a valid sign of
this covenant, may not be performed before the eighth
day of life (counting the day of birth, remembering that
Jewish days begin at night), although it may be delayed
as necessary if the baby is ill. It must also be performed
by a *mohel*, a specialist in ritual circumcision, who is
occasionally a physician, as well. The actual physical
procedure as performed by a *mohel* may be done dif-
ferently from the procedure as performed in the hospital.
For example, circumcisions performed in hospitals usually involve placing a circular clamp around the penis,
whereas these types of instruments are not used by
mohels.

The Infant Must Be Healthy
to Be Circumcised

The performance of ritual circumcision has always been,
in the Sages' days as well as in modern times, contingent
on the health of the child.

Come and hear what Rabbi Hiyya bar Abba stated in the name of Rabbi Yohanan: It once happened with four sisters at Sepphoris that when the first had circumcised her child he died; the second [circumcised her son] and he died; the third [circumcised her son] and he died. The fourth came before Rabban Shimon ben Gamaliel who told her, "Do not circumcise [the boy]."

. . . In the case of circumcision, one can well understand [why the operation is dangerous with some children and not others] since there are families with weak blood [who bleed profusely] and there are families with thick blood [who bleed little]. (*B. Yebamot* 64b)

This passage refers only to prohibiting circumcisions if the mother's sisters had sons with bleeding. This specific prohibition suggests that the Sages were aware of X-linked inheritance, long before chromosomes were known to exist. Presumably the Sages were referring to classical hemophilia (factor 8 deficiency), which, like Duchenne's muscular dystrophy (described in the previous chapter), is an X-linked disease and is carried by healthy women who have two X chromosomes, one with the normal genetic code and one with the hemophilia deficit, and transmitted only to their sons who have one Y chromosome and one X chromosome, which contains the genetic defect that causes hemophilia. Any brothers of the carriers who did not actually have the disease would not be carriers (they have normal X and Y chromosomes). Therefore, their sons could not inherit the disease and could be circumcised.

More obvious signs of illness also precluded the timely performance of a circumcision:

Samuel said: Even if a fever took hold of him for one hour, if the child has a feverish condition, one delays [the circumcision] for thirty days. (*Y. Yebamot* 8:1, 9a)

This is only one of several admonishments that ensure that only healthy boys will be circumcised, a view held today and reiterated in medical opinions regarding circumcision. It is interesting that the Sages use a fever in a baby as an example of illness. Because infants in the first month of life cannot tell us very readily that they are sick, pediatricians today consider a fever to be an indicator of a potentially severe illness. If a baby has a fever (especially a temperature greater than approximately 100.6° Fahrenheit) at any time in the first month of life, many pediatricians admit the baby to the hospital and begin treatment with intravenous antibiotics. It is better to be cautious and treat some babies who eventually are found not to have serious infections than to delay treating a febrile infant until his illness worsens. So, like Samuel, pediatricians today consider a fever in an infant as a potentially serious condition that might require delaying circumcision.

Circumcision: Modern Views

Jewish parents today are faced with conflicting, and often vehemently expressed, opinions regarding circumcision. Most non-Jewish boys are circumcised in the hospital within the first 48 hours of life by the obstetrician/family practitioner who delivered them. Generally, the infant is watched for at least a few hours after the circumcision and then discharged with his family.

> *While I am aware that, in the past, Jewish parents complained that it took some effort to keep their sons from being "accidentally" circumcised in the hospital, I think this is currently much less of a problem. I certainly cannot speak regarding every physician, but I*

believe that relatively little pressure is now placed on parents (Jewish and non-Jewish) by physicians to circumcise their newborns for medical reasons (some physicians are opposed to circumcision). Most non-Jewish parents decide based on personal preference (e.g., whether the boy's father was circumcised) and what they have heard from their friends or discussed with their physicians. [SAA]

In 1989 the Task Force on Circumcision of the American Academy of Pediatrics (AAP) reviewed recent evidence demonstrating certain medical benefits from circumcision. As this is an extremely important issue for Jewish families, the conclusion will be quoted in its entirety. Some medical explanations have been added in parentheses within the AAP statement.

Properly performed newborn circumcision prevents phimosis (narrowing of the foreskin so it can not be retracted properly) and balanoposthitis (inflammation of the glans and upper portion of the penis) and has been shown to decrease the incidence of cancer of the penis among U.S. men. It may result in a decreased incidence of urinary tract infection. However, in the absence of well-designed prospective studies, conclusions regarding the relationship between urinary tract infections to circumcision are tentative. An increased incidence of cancer of the cervix has been found in sexual partners of uncircumcised men infected with human papillomavirus. Evidence concerning the association of sexually transmitted diseases and circumcision is conflicting.

Newborn circumcision is a rapid and generally safe procedure when performed by an experienced operator. It is an elective procedure to be performed only if an in-

fant is stable and healthy. Infants respond to the procedure with transient behavioral changes.

Local anesthesia (dorsal penile nerve block—an injec-
tion given in the base of the penis that numbs the entire
area) may reduce the observed physiologic response (i.e.,
pain/crying) to newborn circumcision. It also has its own
inherent risks. However, reports of extensive experience
or follow-up with the technique in newborns are lacking
(note that more experience has been reported with this
technique since 1989).

Newborn circumcision has potential medical benefits
and advantages as well as disadvantages and risks. When
circumcision is being considered, the benefits and risks
should be explained to the parents and informed consent
obtained.

Circumcision by a *Mohel* Today

No Jewish parents should feel that they are exposing their
son to an increased risk by having him circumcised by a
qualified *mohel*. The pain is transitory and some *mohels*
use local anesthesia, which, as the AAP statement suggests, may decrease the pain. We believe that the likelihood of complication from the procedure is small compared to the benefit of preserving the child's place in the
Jewish tradition. There is no significant scientific evidence
that circumcision causes long-term trauma to the child's
psychological development or affects his sexual ability.
No reputable *mohel* would refuse to perform a circumcision on a Jewish baby due to the inability of the family to
pay. Although there is evidence to suggest it has some

medical benefits, circumcision is performed on Jewish babies as part of our tradition, not because of a compelling medical necessity.

> *Having watched circumcisions done by both obstetricians and* mohels, *we highly recommend that the procedure be performed by a* mohel. *For healthy babies, there is no reason to have it performed in the hospital rather than on the eighth day at home by a* mohel. *As noted above, there are certain medical conditions that require postponing the circumcision or arranging that it be done in consultation with a urologist. These are well known to qualified* mohels *and include prematurity, any potential illness in the baby, and any malformations of the genital system.* [SAA, JZA]

Concluding Thoughts on Newborn Care

Though much has changed from the Sages' day regarding the care of newborns, the basics remain unchanged: keep them warm, dry, clean, fed, and held. Their basic needs are simple. It is when medical intervention is required that the situation becomes more complicated but, thankfully, we have more information at our disposal than the Sages did and can provide more care for infants now than was possible in the rabbinic era.

> *In the end, it is comforting to remember that newborns have very limited needs. If they are fed, changed, kept warm, and held, they will probably be comfortable. With one's first child, just providing these four things*

may seem daunting. However, with subsequent children, the newborn phase seems one of the easiest. After all, when you put a one-month old somewhere, you know that's where they'll stay! Of course, there is the problem of how to feed, cuddle or play with the baby while going to the bathroom. [JZA, SAA]

6

Infant Nutrition

Much of medical writing in ancient times regarding child care focused on ensuring adequate nutrition for infants. The Sages clearly recognized how important it was for infants to be breast-fed and tried to ensure that nursing was maintained. They also took into account how nursing would affect the life of the infant's family. It is worth remembering that modern infant formulas and sanitation were unknown in this era and the Sages' rulings mandating breast-feeding undoubtedly were related to their recognition that artificially fed infants (e.g., cow's milk or goat's milk fed) were less likely to thrive or even survive.

Ancient Beliefs about Breast Milk

To understand breast-feeding in ancient times, we must appreciate a bit about ancient beliefs regarding breast milk.

Rabbi Meir said: All the nine months that a woman does not see [a menstrual discharge of her] blood, she really should do so; but what does the Holy One, blessed be He, do? He directs it [the blood] upward to her breasts and turns it into milk, so that the fetus may come forth and have food to eat. (*Leviticus Rabbah* 14:3)

Rabbi Meir taught that when a woman became pregnant her menstrual blood turned to milk. This was connected to the ancient belief, held by Aristotle, that the embryo was formed out of menstrual blood. That is, it was believed that conception occurred when the semen mixed with the mother's uterine blood. As menstrual blood was visible, the Sages believed the blood in the uterus to be directly involved in conception and lactation. They, like the Greeks, believed that the mammary glands were connected to the uterus and the menstrual blood was diverted from the uterus to the breasts.[1]

These ideas are part of ancient beliefs about gender that equated male and female bodies, their main difference being that male reproductive organs were external and those same organs in women were internal. Naturally, we see in this explanation of how human milk is produced an attempt to explain why pregnant and nursing women generally do not menstruate. It helps illustrate the vast difference between our knowledge and the state of the Sages' medical knowledge.

Nursing in Public

Although we understand that breast-feeding is natural, publicly nursing infants may embarrass some mothers or the people around them. Interestingly, our sources address this topic and it is there that we begin our consideration of Jewish views toward infant nutrition.

> "Who would have said unto Abraham, that Sarah should have given children suck? For I have borne him a son in his old age" (Genesis 21:7). . . . Our mother Sarah was too modest. Abraham our father said to her: "This is not a time for modesty, but uncover your breasts so that all may know that the Holy One, blessed be He, has begun to perform miracles." She uncovered her breasts and the milk gushed forth as from two fountains. (*Genesis Rabbah* 53:9)

As remarkable as Sarah's giving birth was, the Torah indicates that at the age of 90 she considered her ability to nurse Isaac as equally miraculous. In the midrash regarding this Bible verse, we are told that Sarah was admonished by her husband to nurse Isaac publicly because it was such a wonder that she had milk.

In contrast, Rabbi Meir opined that a woman's nursing in public was crude behavior.

> If she ate in the street, if she quaffed in the street, if she suckled in the street, in every case Rabbi Meir says that she must leave [her husband]. (*B. Gittin* 89a)

This passage is part of a long discussion about the validity of rumors regarding a woman and the effect of those rumors on her marital status. As part of this discussion, the Sages bring up the topic of rumors that attribute "loose" behavior to a woman. Rabbi Meir's view is actually the lenient one in this discussion: the woman actually has to be seen doing something "scandalous" in public, such as eating or nursing. Rabbi Akiba, on the other hand, states:

> She must do so [leave her husband] as soon as gossips who spin in the moon begin to talk about her. (*B. Gittin* 89a)

In this context, Rabbi Meir's views represent a commonly agreed upon definition of behavior that is not appropriate for a woman in public, and nursing is part of that definition. From this perspective, it would seem that the Sages did not favor nursing in public. These two passages, the one from *Genesis Rabbah* and Rabbi Meir's statement in *B. Gittin*, are an example of how our tradition can maintain within it conflicting opinions that are both correct at different times. There are times when one has to nurse in public. There are also times when nursing is a private moment between mother and child. Such moments are especially precious for mothers with other children. Then, nursing time can become a special time to pay attention to the newborn.

It should always be remembered that nursing, though natural, is a skill. Some women have an easier time nursing than others, and most women need at least some instruction in how to do it the first time around. A first-time mother may start to feel a little desperate about nursing when her baby is crying with hunger and she can't figure out how to get her latched on. With a little help these early hurdles can usually be overcome. One consequence of the current practice of discharging mothers and infants from the hospital quite soon after birth is that there is less time to deal with these problems there. Numerous resources are available to help mothers, including private lactation consultants, organizations that promote lactation, other mothers, and, of course, physicians. Some obstetricians and pediatricians are clueless about breast-feeding, but others can provide advice, especially regarding medical issues.

When I come to visit patients in the postpartum unit, I always offer to wait or come back when a new mother is nursing her newborn or pumping milk for her premature baby. Many women appeciate a chance for this privacy, but others prefer to talk while nursing. Several have told me that after giving birth in front of an obstetrician, four nurses, and two pediatricians, privacy while nursing is not their biggest concern! [SAA]

Breast-Feeding: Protection from Infection

How do we feel about breast-feeding today? Medical authorities and nutritionists support breast-feeding as best for mothers and their infants throughout the first year of life (we will discuss later in the chapter how mothers and fathers feel about breast-feeding). There is extensive ongoing research into the benefits of breast-feeding and the nutritional characteristics of human milk.

Studies throughout the world have documented the efficacy of breast-feeding in decreasing the rate of infections in infants. Numerous studies performed in the late nineteenth and early twentieth centuries documented a much greater survival rate of breast-fed infants as compared to artificially fed infants. For example, one study in the United States between 1911 and 1916 demonstrated that infant mortality for breast-fed infants was 76 per 1,000 versus 255 per 1,000 for formula-fed infants. Currently, infant mortality is much lower, and the use of antibiotics to combat infections has made it difficult to see such dramatic effects on survival from breast-feeding. Nonetheless, in countries without modern sanitation and with poor access to medical care, recent studies have shown infant mortality to be greater in artificially fed infants.[2]

Recent epidemiological studies have emphasized the value of breast milk in preventing infections and illnesses in infants. For example, one study showed that breast-feeding provided substantial protection against a severe, frequently fatal bacterial cause of diarrhea in young children in underdeveloped countries, preventing about two-thirds of expected cases throughout the first 3 years of life.[3] Numerous studies in the United States over the past 30 years have also shown lower incidences of infections such as diarrhea and respiratory infections in breast-fed infants.

> *In the past, it was generally recommended that infants with diarrhea be taken off all foods except clear liquids. Currently, there is a greater tendency to encourage continued careful feeding, especially breast-feeding, during mild episodes of vomiting and diarrhea.* [SAA]

How Does Breast Milk Protect against Infections?

Much of the current research has focused on *how* breast milk decreases the risk of infection and enhances the growth and development of the infant. Several proteins that are unique to breast milk and that probably have antiinfectious properties have been identified and are being studied. Among these are antibodies (secretory IgA) that attach to the cells lining the airways and the gut and may prevent infectious agents from gaining access to these areas. Furthermore, it appears that the mother is able to selectively secrete into her milk antibodies directed at specific infectious agents in her own, and therefore her infant's, environment.

Another protein, called lactoferrin, is present in large amounts in human milk and is virtually absent in cow's milk. Lactoferrin is believed to prevent excess iron from being used by undesired bacteria or fungi, thereby inhibiting their growth, and permitting fewer infections. Lactoferrin also appears to enhance the growth and development of the intestinal cells.

Are Breast-Fed Babies Bigger? Smarter?

It has been well recognized that most of the nutrients in breast milk are more easily absorbed into the body than those of formula or cow's milk. Surprisingly, however, growth, especially weight gain, may appear to slow down in breast-fed infants around the third or fourth month of life. The apparent slowdown occurs because pediatricians' growth charts were generated during the 1950s when few infants were breast-fed. It appears that especially after the third month of life, formula-fed infants tend to eat more and gain weight more quickly than breast-fed infants. It has been demonstrated that breast-fed infants use energy more efficiently than formula-fed infants, (i.e., they need to take in fewer calories for activity and weight gain) but, despite this, their lower calorie intake causes them to grow a bit more slowly. There is no evidence, however, that the slower growth of breast-fed infants is harmful, and we suspect the correct question isn't "Is there something wrong with breast-fed babies' growth?" but "Are formula-fed babies growing too fat?"

There is uncertainty about whether human milk–fed babies are smarter than formula-fed babies. Several studies have suggested this might be the case, including a very recent study involving premature infants. This remains an area of great controversy that is unlikely to be resolved soon. If there is an intellectual benefit to receiving breast milk, it is probably small. However, ongoing research has shown, for example, that certain fats used for brain development are present in breast milk and not in cow's milk or in current formulas derived from cow's milk. This fact suggests that a developmental benefit from breast milk is possible, albeit far from proven.[4]

One other remarkable characteristic of breast milk is that the iron in it is absorbed far better than the iron in cow's milk or formula. It is therefore unnecessary to provide iron supplements for most breast-fed infants during the first 6 months of life. At that time, iron-fortified cereals can be added.

It is important that formula-fed infants receive iron-fortified formula. There is no evidence that the iron in formula leads to an increased incidence of colic or constipation, and iron deficiency can occur in infants fed low-iron formula. Iron deficiency, which can lead to developmental delays, remains a significant problem for infants in the United States. I would prefer it if low-iron formulas were available only by prescription—there is little reason for their use. It is interest-

ing that the special formulas for infants with feeding problems, such as soy-based and specially predigested formulas, all contain iron fortification; it just isn't marked as obviously on the labels.

The most severe cases of iron deficiency anemia can occur in infants routinely given large amounts of whole cow's milk during the first 6 months of life. In addition to the poor absorption of what little iron is in cow's milk, there may be loss of blood in the stools of infants fed cow's milk, which worsens the iron deficiency. [SAA]

Nutrition for the Lactating Woman

Proper nutrition for the nursing woman, which allows her to maintain an adequate supply of milk for her infant, was a topic of interest in the Sages' era, as it is today. However, we have different ideas about what constitutes a proper diet for a nursing mother than the Sages did.

She [the nursing woman] should not eat bad things while she is with him [i.e., nursing him]. What are these?—Rav Kahana said: For instance, *k'shut* (a reddish clay), sprouts of grain, small fishes and earth. Abaye said: Even pumpkins and quinces. Rav Papa said: Even a palm's heart and unripe dates. Rav Ashi said: Even *kamka* (a sauce with milk in it) and fish-hash. Some of these cause the flow of milk to stop while others cause the milk to become turbid. (*B. Ketubot* 60b)

Obviously, the diet of Babylonian women 1,500 years ago was quite different from our diet today. The Greek physician Soranus (2nd century c.e.) also provided details of the appropriate diet for nursing women:

She [a wet nurse] ought to forgo leek and onions, garlic, preserved meat or fish, radish, and all preserved food and most vegetables [because they are watery and not nourishing]. Rather, she should partake of pure bread, the yolk of eggs, brain, thrushes, the young of pigeons and domestic birds, fishes living among rocks, bass and the meat of suckling pigs.

Current research into nutrition for breast-feeding mothers centers less on omitting potentially harmful substances (mothers need only to avoid foods that cause the baby a problem), and more on assuring an adequate intake of basic nutrients that will provide for the best possible milk for the infant and the most optimal nutrition for the mother.

Where food is in short supply, inadequate nutrition normally causes a decrease in the volume of mother's milk rather than a decrease in its nutritional quality. Supplementing an underfed mother's food intake leads to an increase in the volume of milk she produces and an increased weight gain in the infant. However, this response is not universal and some of the extra food is used by the underfed mother's body for its own energy needs.

In addition to making sure she has adequate nutrition, a nursing mother should also forgo smoking. Recent studies have shown that maternal smoking markedly reduces the quantity (and caloric content) of breast milk.

Maternal smoking also decreases the number of years the infant will have her mother around. It never ceases to amaze me the number of women whose first act in the postpartum ward is to light up a cigarette. I make the new mothers put out the cigarettes before I talk to them about their babies. [SAA]

Maintaining Adequate
Nutrition While Nursing

One of the questions lactating mothers most frequently ask is "May I reduce my caloric intake in order to lose weight while I am nursing?" Some studies of lactating women who dieted suggest that reducing caloric intake slightly below recommended levels was acceptable for losing weight as it still permitted adequate milk production.[5] On the other hand, other recent studies have suggested that protein intake may be marginal in some nursing mothers who are also dieting. Therefore, great caution should be used regarding dieting while nursing.

One area in which I have personally been involved is the study of lactating mothers' need for extra calcium. A significant amount of calcium is secreted in breast milk and the mother must provide for that as well as ensure that her own bones are not depleted of calcium. Ongoing research indicates that some of the calcium in breast milk comes not from a woman's daily intake but from her bones. In other words, lactation is associated with a small loss of maternal bone calcium. Remarkably, however, it appears that after lactation, the woman regains the lost calcium. There is no suggestion that women who have nursed are at an increased risk for osteoporosis. Until further studies are completed, most experts in the field emphasize the importance of maintaining an adequate calcium intake for lactating women.

Although specific studies of their nutritional needs are under way, at the present time there is no reason to discourage teenage mothers from nursing their infants. In fact, the benefits related to bonding from the nursing relationship may be especially important for adolescent mothers. [SAA]

Night Feedings

Night feedings, or very early morning feedings, are part of the infancy period. Although the father is not directly involved when an infant is exclusively breast-fed, he may bring the baby to mother and/or change her diaper and thereby participate in the child's care. As the following passage suggests, since the earliest days, this has been a great time for marital conversation (although "conversation" in this context may be a metaphor for marital relations). In fact, the Sages recognized this situation and used it as a standard way of telling time.

> When the woman talks with her husband and the child sucks from the breast of the mother, let him [the husband] rise and recite [the Shema]. (B. *Berachot* 3a)

This passage is part of a discussion about when one may appropriately recite the Shema. The system of counting time in the ancient world was quite different from ours. Each day and night was divided into 12 "hours" no matter what season it occurred in. Therefore, the length of an hour depended on the season of the year. There are three "watches" each day and each night, or six altogether in one day. How was one to know that the last watch of the nighttime was over and that the first watch of the daytime, when the Shema is recited, had come? When a husband and wife began talking and the infant nurses, it was time for the Shema.

It would be wonderful if night feedings or early morn-
ing feedings were a time of deep and warm commu-
nication between husband and wife. However, it is
probably more often the case that the conversation
consists of the follow terse exchanges:
   "The baby's crying."
   "You get her."
   "I changed her last diaper . . . you get her."
   "Shall we try scissors, rock, paper?"
   "Never mind . . . I'll get her." [SAA, JZA]

Can Men Breast-Feed?

The role fathers play in nurturing their children, even
though they cannot nurse them, is important. Apparently,
some men wish to nurse infants, and this may be an expression of a father's feelings of jealousy as he watches
the close relationship develop between his wife and his
child. In the following exposition, a man is depicted as
having the ability to nurse an infant:

> Did Mordecai feed and sustain? Rabbi Yudan said: One
> time he went round to all the wet nurses but could not
> find one for Esther, whereupon he himself nursed her and
> continuously nursed her [thereby feeding and sustaining,
> by feeding once and then continuously feeding in a sus-
> taining way]. R. Berekhiah and R. Abbahu in R. Eleazar's
> name said: Milk came to him and he nursed her [continu-
> ously]. When R. Abbahu taught this publicly, the congre-
> gation laughed. Said he to them: Yet is it not a Mishnah
> (*M. Makhshirin* 6:7): "Rabbi Simeon ben Eleazar said:
> The milk of a male is ritually clean." (*Genesis Rabbah*
> 30:8)

This passage is part of a much longer exposition of a single word in Genesis 6:9; the word *hayah*, "he was." In this long exposition, only a bit of which is cited here, this word is related to that same word found elsewhere in the *Tanach*. The Sages concentrate on five persons to whom this word *hayah* is applied: Noah, Joseph, Moses, Job, and Mordecai, and they suggest that one of the things these men have in common is their ability to feed and sustain others. Thus, Noah fed the inhabitants of the ark (Genesis 6:21), Joseph fed multitudes during the famine in Egypt (Genesis 47:12), Moses fed the Israelites in the wilderness (e.g., Exodus 16:4 and Numbers 11:31–32), and Job fed poor persons (Job 31:17). However, no obvious way that Mordecai fed and sustained others could be found in the Tanach text, and so the Sages hypothesized that he nursed Esther, not just once, but on a sustaining basis, and he never engaged a wet nurse for her, but fed her himself. (Another midrash, Midrash Psalms 22:23, suggests that Mordecai's wife nursed Esther and that Mordecai raised her.) We might find the passage from *Genesis Rabbah* somewhat fanciful and we are apparently not alone: the congregation laughed at the rabbi who taught this lesson. However, he cites the following mishnah that mentions male milk to support his contention.

These [liquids] neither impart uncleanness nor render [produce] susceptive to uncleanness: perspiration, and ill-smelling moisture [pus]; and excrement and blood that issues with them and [any] fluid appertaining to an eight [months' fetus]—Rabbi Yose says, Save its blood [which conveys uncleanness like the blood of a viable child]. . . . Rabbi Shimon ben Elazar says, The milk of a male is clean [and neither acquires uncleanness nor renders produce susceptive to uncleanness]. (*M. Makhshirin* 6:7)

The system of ritual purity and impurity outlined in the Mishnah was extremely complicated and quite elaborate both practically and symbolically. As we have already mentioned, this system classifies those fluids and materials associated with death as impure. So, for example, menstrual blood is deemed impure because it is associated with the lack of new life, a lack of a fetus. Semen is also considered impure unless it is used to create life. A corpse is the most defiling item of all since it epitomizes death. In such a symbolic scheme, perspiration, the fluid coming from an "8-month baby," who was likened to a stone, and similar fluids have no meaning. They were considered irrelevant to the perpetuation of life and so hold no place in the system of ritual cleanness and impurity. Similarly, milk that a male would produce was considered to be inconsequential to the perpetuation of life and was therefore outside the categorization scheme of ritual purity and impurity.

Of course, a male does not normally produce milk. There is a condition, referred to as galactorrhea, that causes men to secrete a very small amount of milklike substance from their breasts. This may be related to a tumor or a hormonal abnormality. Anecdotal reports of men who have received hormone treatments producing milk also exist, but the composition and quantity of such milk are very unlikely to be suitable for infant nutrition.

This passage may reflect that men have felt envious of women's ability to nurse and wished they could do so, too. Even today, it may be frustrating for a father who couldn't wait for his child to emerge into the world so he could develop his own relationship with her only to find that the baby is still spending most of her time with the mother. Of course, the father can

always give the baby breast milk that has been ex-
pressed and saved as a way of participating in feed-
ing. [JZA, SAA]

Paternal Attitudes toward Breast-Feeding

Paternal attitudes toward breast-feeding were a factor
in the success of nursing in the Sages' day, as they are
today.

> If she [the mother] says that she wishes to nurse her child
> and he [the father] says that she shall not nurse it, we
> listen to her, [because] the suffering would be hers. What,
> [however, is the law] where he says that she shall nurse
> [the child] and she says that she will not nurse it? When-
> ever [nursing by the mother] is not the practice of her
> family, of course, we listen to her. (B. *Ketubot* 61a)

The Sages suggest that forcing a mother to stop nursing
would cause her to suffer. This presumably refers to both
the physical discomfort of rapid weaning and the emotional suffering of the mother forcibly separated from her
infant. However, if a woman comes from a family that was
accustomed to hiring wet nurses, this custom is followed.
Here we see a great deal of sensitivity on the Sages' part
in respecting a woman's wishes and family customs with
regard to this very important aspect of mothering.

Who, among American women, chooses to nurse their
children? In part because formula is available free to many
poor women, and in part because of the limited access poor
women have to lactation counseling, relatively few poor
women choose to nurse. Breast-feeding is more common
among college-educated women (in 1987, 73 percent of

college-educated women nursed, compared to 46 percent of women without a college education). However, the need to return to work has led to a situation where fewer than half of those mothers who start out nursing their infants continue nursing more than 6 months.[6]

> The problem of increasing the frequency with which lower-income women breast-feed is not a simple one. It would seem easy, since it's obviously less expensive to breast- than bottle-feed (this is true even if one accounts for the increased food intake needs of nursing mothers). However, given that many lower-income mothers can receive formula for free, this is not much of an incentive. We certainly wouldn't advocate denying free formula to lower-income families. What would that do but hurt the infants? However, more could be done to support lower-income mothers who wish to breast-feed. This support might include increased access to lactation consultants, discounts on breast pump rentals, and educational programs regarding the importance of breast-feeding. [SAA, JZA]

The text clearly indicates that the father may not prevent his wife from nursing. The question is, why would a father object? The Talmud gives no clues to this, other than mentioning family traditions, but current research suggests that fathers' objecting to their wives' nursing is a significant problem even today. In a recent survey of fathers at a prenatal childbirth class, a significant number of the men were concerned that breast-feeding would (1) interfere with sex, (2) make the mother's breasts ugly, or (3) be harmful to the mother's breasts. These complaints were more frequent among fathers whose wives planned to formula feed (40 to 60 percent of these fathers) but were present in 20 to 40 percent of the fathers whose wives planned to partially or wholly breast-feed.[7]

Of these concerns, the second and third represent anxieties that could be discussed and presumably overcome with prenatal education. Regarding the first, numerous previous reports have contained conflicting data regarding sexuality during the period of nursing. Parents need to be aware that the birth of any infant will alter their sexual relationship for a period of time. Lactation does lead to a decrease in vaginal moisture, and nursing mothers should be advised that a lubricant may be necessary. Clearly, fathers need to be part of the breast-feeding education process and these issues need to be addressed in an open fashion.

Breast-Feeding and Contraception

In general, the Sages were concerned lest a woman become pregnant while nursing, and they allowed her to use a contraceptive to forestall this eventuality.

> Three kinds of women have intercourse with a contraceptive device (*mokh*): a girl under age, a pregnant woman, and a nursing mother. . . . A nursing mother—lest she kill her infant. For Rabbi Meir would say, "The entire period of twenty-four months [of nursing] one winnows inside and scatters [seed] outside." And Sages say, "One has intercourse in the normal way, and God will look out for him, as it is said, 'The Lord guards the innocent'" (Psalm 116:6). (*T. Niddah* 2:6)

The Sages' ruling that a nursing woman should use a contraceptive device testifies to the importance they attached to the ability of the mother to nurse for 24 months. As we noted previously, many Sages felt that pregnancy and childbirth would cause the mother's milk to stop and lead to the death of the child.

The Sages apparently were not aware of the contraceptive effect of nursing. Current research has focused on identifying the nature and duration of this effect. For example, one study in women from India showed that nursing for an average of 20 months led to an average of 11 months of amenorrhea (no menstrual periods) and an average birth interval of 24 months.[8]

The use of oral contraceptives does not necessarily require stopping nursing. Oral contraceptives may decrease the amount of milk a mother produces, but usually nursing may be continued safely. It is worth specifically discussing this issue with one's doctor before resuming the pill rather than assuming that this means the end of lactation. There are actually relatively few medications that are absolutely considered reasons for stopping breast-feeding (or at least halting it while the medications are being taken). These include certain blood-thinning agents, anticancer drugs, and "radioactive" drugs (which might be taken as part of diagnostic tests). [SAA]

Does Nursing Prevent Pregnancy?
A Study of Orthodox American Women

Because very few American women use nursing as their sole method of contraception, this has been a difficult topic to study in the United States. To examine the contraceptive effects of nursing in a modern setting, a recent study looked at what may be the only large group of American women who frequently nurse throughout the first year of life without using other forms of contraception: Orthodox Jewish women. In this study, over 100 Orthodox mothers were questioned about their nursing and contraceptive practices. The researchers found that among those who breast-fed, the average length of nursing was 11 months and the average length of amenorrhea (i.e., no menstrual periods) was 9 months. Birth intervals between children averaged 22 months. The researchers compared this group of women to a matched group who formula-fed their infants. The formula-feeding mothers had a mean birth interval of only 16 months (significantly less than the breast-fed infants).[9] In other words, on the average, nursing added about 6 months to the time space between children.

Why is nursing not more widely advertised as a contraceptive? Basically, to be effective, mothers must exclusively nurse with a minimum, or total lack, of formula supplements. Under such conditions, and if the mother remains amenorrheic, nursing is reported to be 98 percent effective in preventing pregnancy during the first 6 months after birth. Although nursing generally increases birth spacing, its effectiveness depends on limiting feeding supplements, which are widely used in the United States. Furthermore, most American women choose other methods of birth control that are effective beyond the first 6 to 12 months after childbirth. Nonetheless, when considering population planning on a worldwide basis, especially in poorer countries, increasing the rate of lactation is an important method of decreasing birth rates. This is one reason (in addition to disease prevention) why formula feeding should not be emphasized in these countries.

How Long to Nurse: The Sages' View

There is considerable discussion in rabbinic literature regarding how long an infant should be nursed. This had important ramifications for the status of the infant, mother, and the family unit. The following passages illustrate some of that discussion.

> A child nurses continuously for twenty-four months. From that age onward [he is to be regarded] as one who sucks an abominable thing: these are the words of Rabbi Eliezer. And Rabbi Joshua says: [He may be breast fed] even for five years continuously. If he ceased [after twenty-four months] and started again he is to be regarded as sucking an abominable thing. (*T. Niddah* 2:3)

Jewish law (*halakhah*) follows Rabbi Joshua's words: a child should be nursed for a minimum of 2 years and weaned by 4 years of age if healthy, 5 years of age if sickly.[10] During the first 2 years of life, a child is allowed to resume nursing after having stopped for a time, but after 2 years of age, once the child stops, she does not return to nursing.

One might ask if it is even *possible* to nurse an infant who has already been weaned. The answer is a qualified yes. Doing so is referred to as relactation and takes a large amount of effort, but is possible. It is even possible for some mothers who have never been pregnant to nurse their adopted children (induced lactation), although supplementation may be required as well as medication to help induce lactation. Not unexpectedly, a strong commitment to nurse will be necessary on the adoptive mother's part.

How Long to Nurse and
Its Implications in Jewish Thought

The amount of time a woman was required to nurse her child had several Jewish legal consequences for her, particularly in terms of her ability to obtain a divorce and remarry. The Sages associated a new pregnancy with a decrease in a woman's milk supply: this was why they permitted her to use the contraceptive device described in *T. Niddah* 2:6. Therefore, they ruled that a nursing mother must nurse for two years before she could remarry, in order to assure that a new pregnancy did not threaten her milk supply, and therefore her baby's survival. However, we learn that there is a conflict among the Sages with regard to the absolute minimum amount of time a woman was to nurse her child.

> [If a man says] here is your *get* (divorce document) on condition that you . . . nurse my child—how long need she nurse him? Two years. Rabbi Judah says, "Eighteen months." (*M. Gittin* 7:6)

Though divorce is the issue under discussion, this passage reveals that there were at least two views on the absolute minimum amount of time a woman should nurse her child.

One other authority (*B. Ketubot* 60b) allows a nursing woman to marry after only 15 months of nursing her child.

However, it is generally accepted that the amount of time a mother should nurse her child is 2 years.

Some Sages were concerned that a mother might commit infanticide in order to be allowed to remarry. However, this concern is rejected as being beyond the pale: infanticide simply was not believed to be practiced by sane Jewish women.

> It once actually happened that a mother strangled her child. This incident is, however, no [proof against remarriage after an infant death]. That woman was insane, for [sane] women do not strangle their children. (B. Ketubot 60b)

In general, in Jewish law, we cannot make law based on what an insane person might do. Here is a case where we see this principle in action. The Sages ruled that infanticide was simply not committed by sane Jewish women. This is how strongly this value was held in the Jewish community: if one did commit infanticide, one was automatically considered insane. Perhaps some desperate or insane women did kill their infants (as today, infants are occasionally abandoned), but we recognize, as did the Sages, that this is not normative behavior.

> *This passage reflects the fact that some women may feel overwhelmed by a newborn's needs and may resent the baby's attachment to them. Obviously, this is not a good situation for mother or child. What to do? First of all, if possible, allow the father to participate in child care as fully as possible. A father can hold a baby right on his chest and rock her, providing the sound of his heartbeat and the skin-to-skin contact that delights infants.*

Just as nursing is a skill that some mothers find easy and some find difficult, staying home with a young child is something that fulfills some women and makes others very unhappy. Children will probably do better with a contented mother who spends some time at work or out of the home than an irrational one who feels chained to the house. God gives each of us gifts and capacities, and we live our lives best when we follow those natural gifts rather than fighting them because someone expects that we should.

The entity of postpartum depression is a real one and occasionally may need appropriate psychological intervention. There is no reason for mothers to feel that sadness in the weeks after birth is something to be ashamed of and/or ignored. [JZA, SAA]

When to Wean: Current Thinking

How do we currently feel about nursing during the second year of life and thereafter? In general, nursing after the first year of life is relatively uncommon in modern American society (less than 10 percent of infants). We note that it is important that weaning be done gradually whenever possible and absolutes as to when it should occur are not based on scientific data. The American Academy of Pediatrics recommends that whole cow's milk not be introduced until at least 6 months of age, but most authorities strongly recommend that formula or human milk be given until at least 12 months of age.

Given these considerations, the question may be "Is it socially acceptable to nurse a toddler?" Many people's instinctive reaction is to recoil at the thought of a breast-feeding toddler and believe this to be abnormal, immoral, or in some way incestuous. This attitude is based on perceptions of impropriety, not reality. Toddlers usually only nurse once or, at most, a few times daily (such as before bedtime) and, as the passages from rabbinic literature suggest, this practice has thousands of years of history behind it. Breast-feeding one's toddler is acceptable under rabbinic law, and there is no reason that it should be criticized today.

Although nursing toddlers is uncommon in the United States, several groups, most notably the La Leche League, strongly support mothers who wish to nurse their older infants and toddlers and provide support services for these mothers. Few would consider it immoral for a toddler to drink cow's milk from a bottle with a nipple, so why should it be a shock that some toddlers wish to nurse?

Weaning Foods: What and When

One area of ongoing research concerns the effects of various weaning foods on an infant's diet. For example, it is commonly taught that cereal should be the first solid food introduced to an infant's diet and that it should be added between 4 and 6 months of age. Common reasons for this include concerns that earlier introduction would decrease milk intake, promote allergies, or decrease absorption into the body of important milk nutrients (including iron and calcium). However, there is little data regarding the functional significance of these concerns, and detailed research has only recently begun to answer the question of what solid foods should be fed an infant and when.

*Starting to feed a baby in a high chair is another one
of those milestones of childhood that is really fun. It's
a time for relating to your baby and playing games
as well as for feeding. One game that our children
developed on their own was trying to feed themselves.
Soon, they would not allow us to help them as they
worked to master this skill. In this process, their hands
and faces and clothes and the chair would become
covered with baby food and Cheerios. The dog would
hover nearby and, to their delight, start licking the
droppings from the floor and chair and, when our
heads were turned, their hands and faces. This is one
of those things that horrifies you with the first baby
and that you take with remarkable aplomb thereafter.*
[SAA, JZA]

Wet Nursing

In ancient days, it was the prerogative of many upper-class
women to hire other women to nurse their children. These
women were referred to as wet nurses. Although this custom, as we discuss below, does not continue to this day,
the use of wet nurses was widespread in ancient times and
is even preferred by Soranus. The Sages, although recognizing that wet nursing was practiced and was acceptable, indicate a preference for maternal nursing, and our
sources discuss rules regarding wet nursing.

The Sages recognized that the bond between an infant
and a nursing mother is an important one. In the following passage, they state that once a mother has com-
menced nursing and the infant has formed such a bond
with her, she may not discontinue nursing.

> An infant who recognizes his mother—they do not give him to a wet nurse because of the danger to life. An infant nurses from a non-Jewish woman and from the unclean cow, and from any of them does he nurse, and even on the Sabbath. (*T. Niddah* 2:5)

The importance the Sages placed on nursing is seen in the ruling that an infant may nurse from a non-Jewish woman or an unclean animal, even on the Sabbath. Nursing was a child's source of sustenance and, as such, its importance overrode Sabbath restrictions. Interestingly, some infants apparently did receive cow's milk.

The Sages also realized that the issue of a woman's milk supply was important, and they worried lest a wet nurse attempt to nurse more than one child at a time.

> Our Rabbis taught: If a woman was given a child to nurse she must not nurse together with it either her own child or the child of any friend of hers. (*B. Ketubot* 60b)

This woman, who is presumably paid a wage to nurse the child, must nurse it exclusively. Perhaps the Sages were concerned that the nursing woman might not be fair in distributing the milk between the infants. They may also have been concerned that the wet nurse would not produce enough milk for both infants.

Providing Care for an Infant

One of a parent's most serious responsibilities is finding good child care. Even a parent who does not work outside the home, or one who works only part time, must find appropriate babysitters. When do the Sages feel that a parent, in this case the mother, is no longer obligated to care exclusively for her child? When the child is finished nursing, that is, 2 years.

> A woman is obligated to care (*tippul*) for her child for the entire twenty-four months. Whether it is her child or whether it was a child given to her to nurse, the woman who is given a child to nurse should not do work [while caring] for him and should not suckle another child with him. (*T. Niddah* 2:4)

Can a mother let someone else care for her infant? The word in our first sentence is *tippul*, which indicates that the woman is obligated to care for her own child for 24 months. This passage goes on to use the term for nursing. It is possible that the first sentence refers only to nursing, but it is also possible that it means that the mother is responsible for nursing as well as general child care for 24 months. The Sages also believed that undue expenditure of energy or work was a mortal danger because it could hurt the child's milk supply; her main source of nutrition (*T. Niddah* 2:5). The Sages here seem to indicate that a woman should not do additional, stressful work while she nurses, that is, for 2 years.

Should a mother return to work before her child is 2 years old? Should she care for the infant herself, as the first sentence of this Toseftan passage suggests, even if she is not nursing the child? The passage requiring the mother to care for her infant could be interpreted as requiring that the mother ensure her child is in a safe, nurturing environment, even if she is not physically present. Obviously, there are no absolute answers to this question and parents must decide what is best for them and their child. Yet equally obviously, children must be provided with adequate love and care in the first 2 years of life.

Although the Sages' apparent solution is that the mother not work for 2 years after childbirth or that she find a wet nurse, these are not practical solutions today for most families. Many mothers return to work soon after their infants' births. In 1990, 53 percent of all mothers (68 percent of college graduates) with children younger than 1 year were working, up from 38 percent in 1980. Many mothers are able to successfully combine the two (that is, by pumping and saving milk during breaks at work) and report that the continuation of breast-feeding while working provides them with great satisfaction and helps them maintain the closeness of the nursing relationship with their infant.[11] For others, continuing to nurse after resuming work is not practical or desired, and these mothers are to be supported in their decision. It's hard enough having to leave one's 6-week-old to go to work without also being made to feel guilty about weaning. Those mothers who decide not to continue nursing after returning to work may feel guilty unnecessarily. Certainly in Western countries, most infants will grow and thrive on currently available formulas.

I strongly recommend that families discuss formula choices with their pediatrician or health care provider, rather than follow advice from television commercials. All formula companies strive to produce formulas that contain nutrients that are as similar as possible to those provided by human milk and will be well tolerated by infants. Claims that any one formula is more like breast milk than its competitors or is better at preventing allergies are dubious at best.

Finding adequate child care can be difficult. It may take a good bit of effort to find a person or institution whose values you feel you share with regard to a child's needs. The usual guidelines to hiring anyone apply to this: do research, check references, and explore multiple options before deciding. [SAA]

Cross-Nursing, or Sharing Human Milk

Although wet nursing is no longer practiced in Western countries, the exchange of milk between a mother and someone else's infant is likely to take place in one of two situations. The first may occur when friends or relatives nurse each other's babies (or share bottled human milk). The second occurs when milk is obtained from a breast milk bank, which exists to provide human milk to babies with special needs (such as premature infants or babies with a severe intolerance of formula) who cannot receive their own mothers' milk. When practicing cross-nursing one must be cautious, since a few cases of HIV infection in infants have been associated with transmission from human milk.

Concluding Thoughts on Infant Nutrition

In this chapter we emphasized the value of nursing for two reasons. First, this was the only sort of infant nutrition the Sages knew, and therefore our sources naturally concentrate on this form of feeding. Second, breast-feeding is currently recommended for infants and we wanted to convey why this is so. However, we want to reemphasize that mothers should not feel guilty if they do not wish to nurse or cannot do so. Nursing can be a difficult skill to learn, and some mothers may naturally do it quite well while others may find it more difficult. As long as an infant is adequately fed and nurtured, the parents have discharged their duty to the child.

7

Developmental Stages of Childhood

The development of our children, the strides they make after entering this world, are daily miracles—and trials —that form the fabric of our lives. Once a child has completed the first years of life, our thoughts turn to schooling, discipline, and our ability as parents to inculcate in our children the values we hold dearest. The Sages were as concerned with these issues as we are. And because learning was so central to their lives and was, for them, a form of spirituality, they said a great deal about developmental issues from which we can gain insight.

Cognitive and Spiritual Developmental Stages

When should a child begin school? When is a child "ahead" or "behind" in his studies? A classic text that

prescribes norms for learning and achievement comes
from the Mishnah text, Pirkei Avot.

> [Judah ben Tema] used to say, "At five years [the age is
> reached for the study of] Bible, at ten [for the study of]
> Mishnah, at thirteen for the [fulfillment of the] command-
> ments, at fifteen for [the study of] Talmud, at eighteen
> for marriage, at twenty for seeking [a livelihood], at thirty
> for [full] strength, at forty for understanding, at fifty for
> [giving] counsel, at sixty a man attains old age, at sev-
> enty white old age, at eighty rare old age, at ninety he
> is bending over the grave, at a hundred he is as if he
> were already dead and had passed away from the world.
> (*M. Pirkei Avot* 5:24)

Here we have a timeline for Jewish studies that could still
be appropriately applied today. First, we begin teaching
our young children Bible stories. There are numerous
excellent storybooks that tell Bible tales in an attractively
presented manner and that we can begin reading to our
children. After all, we can as easily read about David and
Goliath as about the Cookie Monster. At the age of 10,
we begin studying Mishnah with our children. The Mishnah
is presented in clear, elegant Hebrew in simple, logical
form. It is ideal for teaching Hebrew and the basics of
Jewish practice. Of course, it can also be studied in En-
glish translation. (Ideally one would pick a tractate with
more, rather than less, modern-day significance, such as
Berachot or *Megillah*, rather than a tractate on, for example, the Temple sacrifices.)

> *The curriculum this mishnah provides is only a tex-*
> *tual one. We start a child's Jewish education long*
> *before the age of 5 by observing the* mitzvot *ourselves*

*and making these part of the foundation of family life.
For example, our 2-year-old daughter loves to watch
me light candles on Friday night and cover my eyes.
She may see it as merely a variation on a game of
peekaboo, but these memories will become part of her
definition of what kind of place the world is. It's a place
where we light candles once a week. Later, she'll learn
why, but her assumption will always be that we do it.*
[JZA]

The custom of giving a child independence and responsibility at 13 years of age (12 for girls) is a wise one: just
when a child is itching for freedom—we give it to him! In
addition, just when a child can be at his most difficult to
deal with, the preparations for the *bar* (or *bat*) *mitzvah*
ceremony give him a focus for his energies and allow him
to do something for which he can receive great praise.
We should note, however, that the *bar* or *bat mitzvah*
ceremony has become a life-cycle event for the entire
family and is a chance for that family to face itself and
affirm the changing identity of at least one of its members. Particularly when there has been a divorce (and
often, remarriage) the *bar* or *bat mitzvah* forces a clari-
fication of new roles on everyone's part and a renegotia-
tion of whatever arrangements were made at the time of
the divorce.

Bar and bat mitzvah *celebrations, unfortunately, are
often inappropriately lavish affairs, offered in a spirit
of competition with other families, rather than moments of celebration of a child's Jewish learning. Some
families even go deeply into debt in order to offer their
children the "party of their dreams." The* bar *or* bat
mitzvah *then becomes a statement of how well-off the*

*parents are: a ceremonial display of wealth instead of
wisdom. How much better off our children would be
if, instead of spending tens of thousands of dollars on
a party, families would focus on the ceremony itself,
the achievement, Jewishly speaking, of their child. If
the family must spend large sums of money to cele-
brate the occasion, they could take a trip together to
Israel, or make a significant donation to their synagogue or other charity.* [JZA, SAA]

Once children become responsible for their own performance of the *mitzvot*, the next step for them is to continue their Jewish education with the study of the Talmud.
In other words, their Jewish education does not stop after
the *bar* or *bat mitzvah* ceremony. The Talmud provides
insight and intellectual challenge for teenagers in need of
guidance regarding the difficult issues they face: relationships with the opposite sex, assimilation, and the like.
Once a child has become a competent Jew, then this
mishnah teaches that he is ready for marriage and the
pursuit of a career. One of the lessons of this mishnah
seems to be that a solid foundation of Jewish learning is
a prerequisite for living a successful and fulfilling life.

The Four Sons: Stages of Childhood

Another very famous passage that has to do with children
may be interpreted as a paradigm for a child's development. The Haggadah, which is read at the Passover seder
(the festive meal that celebrates the exodus from Egypt),
is largely a collection of teachings from rabbinic literature.
The description of the four sons in the Haggadah could
be seen either as a description of four different children

or as a description of the same child going through developmental phases, beginning with a mature teenager, then a younger, rebellious teen, then a child, and, finally, a very young child.

> The Torah alludes to four types of children: one who is wise, and one who is wicked, one who is simple and one who does not know how to ask.
>
> What does the wise child ask? "What are the statutes, the laws and the ordinances which Adonai our God has commanded us?" (Deuteronomy 6:20). You should inform this child of all the laws of Pesach, including the ruling that nothing should be eaten after the *afikomen*.
>
> What does the wicked child ask? "What does this ritual mean to *you*?" (Exodus 12:26). To "you" and not to "him." Since he removes himself from the community by denying God's role in the Exodus, set his teeth on edge [i.e., shake him up] by replying, "This is done because of what God did for *me* when I went out of Egypt" (Exodus 13:8). "For me." Not for him. Had he been there, he would not have been redeemed.
>
> What does the simple child ask? "What is this all about?" You should tell him, "It was with a mighty hand that Adonai took us out of Egypt, out of the house of bondage" (Exodus 13:14).
>
> As for the child who does not know how to ask, you should open the discussion for him, as it is written, "And you shall explain to your child on that day, 'It is because of what Adonai did for me when I went free out of Egypt'" (Exodus 13:8). (*Y. Pesachim* 10:4, 37d)[1]

At some point in his life, a child will probably go through the four phases mentioned in this passage: not knowing enough about the Jewish tradition to ask about it, knowing enough to ask simple questions, being rebellious and rejecting the tradition and, finally, having the intellectual and emotional maturity to be interested in Judaism for himself.

This passage from the Haggadah is based on the fact that there are four times when children are told, or ask about, the Exodus in the Torah:

> When your son asks you in time to come, saying: What mean the testimonies, and the statutes and the ordinances, which the Lord your God has commanded you? then you shall say to your son: We were Pharaoh's bondsmen in Egypt; and the Lord brought us out of Egypt with a mighty hand. (Deuteronomy 6:20-21)
>
> And it shall come to pass, when your children shall say unto you: What mean you by this service? that you will say: It is the sacrifice of the Lord's passover, that He passed over the houses of the children of Israel in Egypt, when he smote the Egyptians, and delivered our houses. (Exodus 12:26-27)
>
> And it shall be when your son asks you in time to come, saying: What is this? that you shall say unto him: By strength of hand the Lord brought us out from Egypt, from the house of bondage. (Exodus 13:14)
>
> And you shall tell your son in that day, saying: It is because of that which the Lord did for me when I came forth out of Egypt. (Exodus 13:8)

We can see why the Sages matched the different Torah passages to the four stages of childhood. Deuteronomy 6:20-21 is the sophisticated question of an older, more learned, child. Exodus 12:26-27 is the question of a child separating from his parents, asking why this was done "for you" not "for us" or "for me." The simple question "What is this?" comes from a younger child whose curiosity is piqued by the preparations for the seder, and Exodus 13:8 portrays a parent simply telling a child about the Exodus and records no asking on the child's part, as would be the case for a toddler.

The Haggadah helps explain how we should deal with our children at different stages in their development. We should tailor our answers to their questions and needs. The Haggadah also demands of parents that we be knowledgeable enough to teach our children the details of the Jewish tradition when they have grown to the point at which they are able to appreciate them.

How can we keep our children from rejecting their Judaism and doing other self-destructive things? How do we prevent them from exploring other religions, drugs, or sex? With its response to the wicked son, this passage from the Haggadah suggests that when our children are rebellious and tempted to reject their Judaism, we should respond strongly that this is undesirable behavior that will have definite, strong, negative consequences. (A similar passage in the Yerushalmi makes the evil son sound more contemptuous, more like a rebellious teenager. There, he says, "What is this sacrifice to you? Why do you go to all this effort year after year to sacrifice [the passover lamb]?") In addition, by inculcating in our children a sense of self-esteem and a love of Judaism in the first two phases of life mentioned in this passage, we may "inoculate" them, as it were, against doing the most self-destructive things in adolescence. And no matter how pugnacious they may become, we still include them: the evil son is, after all, still at the seder.

Finally, this passage suggests that parents must be knowledgeable enough about Judaism to answer the sophisticated questions of an older child. So often, Jews abandon their Jewish education after their *bar* or *bat mitzvah* and are consequently stuck with a child's view of the religion. Judaism is a sophisticated system of practice and belief that can satisfy both children's and adults' spiritual needs. However, to satisfy an adult's needs, it must be apprehended on an adult level. This passage seems to demand that parents take responsibility for leading themselves, and their children, to this highest level of knowledge.

> *Few forms of Jewish education have a greater impact than spending time in Israel. Whether you are an adult, teenager, or child, your Jewish identity will be stronger for having spent even a short amount of time in Israel. Just being in a place where most of the people you see on the street are Jewish and the signs and newspapers are in Hebrew is tremendously exciting.* [SAA, JZA]

"Clay Pots Sure Look Great Smashed against the Wall, Dad"

The Sages were well aware that children need to be allowed to explore and that they may be somewhat destructive as they learn about their world:

> Abaye said: Mother told me the proper treatment for a child consists in [bathing it in] warm water and [rubbing it with] oil. If he has grown a bit, [feed him] an egg with *kutah* [a preserve consisting of sour milk, bread crusts, and salt]; if he grows up still more, the breaking of clay vessels. Thus did Rabbah buy clay vessels in damaged condition for his children who would break them. (*B. Yoma* 78b)

When raising young children, some sacrifices in elegance may have to be made. It may not be the most opportune period in one's life for using fine china each night. Better to have a less elegant environment than to constantly be saying no to an exploring infant or toddler. Our wedding china sits gathering dust in a remote closet of the house, until the day when we feel our children won't be tempted to see how nice it looks in pieces. [JZA, SAA]

What is interesting here is that a great Sage is so involved in the raising of his children that he buys appropriate toys for them. There are several important modern examples of parents buying toys for children before they are ready for them. One example is the infant walker. It's so cute to see little 6-month-old infants roaming the house in their walker . . . and right down the stairs! The American Medical Association recently issued a report noting the potential severity of walker-related injuries. Over 90 percent of all stairwell injuries among infants in the first year of life are related to walkers.[2] When children are ready to walk, they will. Until then, crawling is fine.

Similarly, the American Academy of Pediatrics issued a "position statement" several years ago regarding skateboarding accidents. One statement therein is that "children under 5 years old should not ride skateboards."[3] Talk about an age-inappropriate toy! That seems almost comparable to the Federal Aviation Authority stating that "toddlers should not fly jet aircraft."

There is much to be said for letting children develop at their own pace, letting them accomplish things when they feel ready to do so and want to do so themselves. After all, to succeed in life they will have to want to fulfill themselves and be in touch with their own feelings rather than their parents' wishes and feelings. As many a mother has remarked when asked when her child will stop sucking his thumb/using a pacifier/wearing diapers, "I'm sure he'll have stopped by the time he gets to college."

When I was a medical student there was a little boy in the hospital (for a different reason) whose pediatrician decided it was time for him to stop sucking his thumb. So he ordered the nurses and residents to paint the thumb with a sour solution to discourage thumb sucking. This was dutifully done each morning in time for the pediatrician's daily visits. At night, the residents would wash the stuff off. Eventually, the pediatrician caught on and gave up.

There remain many parents, pediatricians, and others who believe in strict schedules for weaning, for sleeping through the night, for toilet training. I do not concur. Perhaps it is because I was an incompletely toilet-trained kindergartener who managed to make it through MIT anyway, but I refuse to believe that absolute rules regarding weaning or toilet training are useful. That doesn't mean one can't do a little pushing at times, but nothing magic happens on the second birthday that makes diapers a sign of a bad child or parents. [SAA]

Make Sure They Have a Good Breakfast, Too

We are all aware that it's important for children to have a good breakfast before going to school. Hungry children can hardly be expected to concern themselves with schoolwork. The Sages were aware of this, and, in the following wonderful passage, discuss the importance of breakfast.

Our rabbis taught: Thirteen things were said of the morning bread: It is an antidote against heat and cold, winds and demons; instills wisdom into the simple, causes one to triumph in a lawsuit, enables one to study and teach the Torah, to have his words heeded, and retain scholarship, he [who partakes therefore] does not perspire, lives with his wife and does not lust after other women and it kills the worms in one's intestines. Some say, it also expels jealousy and induces love. (B. Baba Metsia 107b)

Somehow, it's difficult to think of a blueberry muffin as an aid to marital fidelity, or as an anti-helminth (worm medicine), but it's hard to argue with the idea that eating breakfast is important. This passage may allude to the belief that a person who is able to satisfy his bodily needs may well be able to perform his day's work more successfully than someone who is hungry or so disorganized that he skips breakfast.

While, in general, breakfast is a good thing, we needn't force children to eat specific items. One acquaintance of mine was forced to eat oatmeal each morning for breakfast and would invariably throw it up on her way to school. Her mother stopped forcing it on her only when she realized she was simply wasting the oatmeal. Better to allow a child to choose from a variety of healthy alternatives for breakfast than force one choice on him. [JZA]

When Should Children Begin Observing Judaism?

Parents often wonder when and how they should start to teach their children to observe Judaism. The Sages not only give us an answer, they even give us the syllabus for introducing young children to Jewish practice.

> Mishnah: A minor who knows how to shake [the *lulav*, i.e., the four plant species waved together on the holiday of Sukkot] is subject to the obligation of *lulav*. Gemara: . . . Our Rabbis taught, A minor who knows how to shake [the *lulav*] is subject to the obligation of the *lulav*; [if he knows how] to wrap himself [with the *tallit*] he is subject to the obligation of *tsitsit*; [if he knows how] to look after *tefillin*, his father acquires *tefillin* for him; if he is able to speak, his father must teach him Torah and the reading of the Shema. What [in this context] could be meant by Torah?—Rav Hamnuna replied, [The Scriptural verse] "Moses commanded us a Law, an inheritance of the congregation of Jacob" (Deuteronomy 33:4). What [in this context] is meant by the reading of the Shema? The first verse (Deuteronomy 6:4). . . . If [a child] can eat an olive size of roast meat, the Passover lamb may be slaughtered on his behalf, as it is said, "According to the eating of every man" (Exodus 12:4). Rabbi Judah says, [This inclusion of the child in the eating party of a Paschal lamb is not allowed] until he is able to pick out an eatable. In what manner?—If he is given a splinter, he throws it away; if he is given a nut, he eats it. (*B. Sukkah* 42b)

When do we start teaching children to observe Judaism? As soon as they show they are ready. When they can shake a *lulav*, we have them shake it. When they can wear *tsitsit* (the ritual fringes on a garment that remind us to observe the commandments), that is, after being toilet trained, they wear them. When they speak, we teach them a line from the Torah (Deuteronomy 33:4) and the first line of the Shema (Deuteronomy 6:4). And when they eat solid foods with the intention of eating those foods, we include them as real participants in the Passover seder.

This last ruling may require a bit of explanation. In ancient days, when the Temple still stood, a group slaughtered a lamb on Passover. This had to be done with the intention to include in this *mitzvah* each individual eating at the seder. Each person, in effect, bought shares in a Passover lamb and all the people who bought shares in one lamb constituted an eating party. Therefore, the Sages wonder, "At how young an age can we include a child in this eating party and thereby become obligated to buy him a share in a lamb?"

It is interesting that the Sages make note of a toddler's propensity to put anything in his mouth. Our children are not the only ones who try to eat sticks and stones: they did it then, too! Indeed, a child's ability to explore with his hands, rather than his mouth, and to discern between edible and inedible objects are important developmental steps. It is not current practice to give peanuts to small children. A peanut is just the right size to fit in a small child's windpipe and choke him.

What should you do if your child eats dirt or the dog's food? Again, you may panic with your first, but you will probably calm down with the second and third children. While it's hardly part of a recommended diet, a little sand or dog food is not going to harm a child unless the dog starts snapping at the child for stealing his food.

These problems may come to the fore particularly during the holiday of Sukkot. Decorating the sukkah, and eating outside in it are tremendous fun. Just make sure your kids don't try to eat the decorations or the grass while they're out there! [SAA, JZA]

Teaching Children to Fast on Yom Kippur

In another passage that addresses the gradual increase in Jewish observance by children, the Sages outline how we teach our children to fast on Yom Kippur.

Mishnah: One should not afflict children [make them fast] at all on the Day of Atonement. But one trains them a year or two before [they reach their majority] in order that they become used to religious observances.

Gemara: Since [the Mishnah has taught already that] two years before [they attain majority] they must be trained, is it necessary to state that one must do so a year before that time?—Rav Hisda said: This is no difficulty: the one [teaching them to fast two years in advance] refers to a healthy child, the other [teaching them to fast one year in advance] to a sickly one.

Rav Huna said: At the age of eight and nine years one trains them by hours, at the age of ten and eleven they must fast to the end of the day by Rabbinic ordinance. At the age of twelve they must fast to the end of the day by Biblical law, [all this] referring to girls. And Rav Nahman said: At the age of nine and ten one trains them by hours, at the age of eleven and twelve they must fast to the end of the day by Rabbinic ordinance, at the age of thirteen they must fast to the end of the day by Biblical law, [all this] referring to boys. And Rabbi Yohanan said: There is no Rabbinic ordinance about the obligation of children to fast to the end of the day. But at the age of ten and eleven one trains them by hours, at the age of twelve they must fast to the end of the day by Biblical law. (B. Yoma 82a)

The opinions of this passages are summarized in the following chart:

Authority	Age for Fasting Hours	Age for Fasting to End of Day (Rabbinic Edict)	Age for Fasting to End of Day (Biblical Edict)
Rav Huna (for girls)	8–9	10–11	12
Rav Nahman (for boys)	9–10	11–12	13
R. Yohanan (boys and girls)	10–11	NA	12

Here we see rabbinic literature's propensity for preserving different traditions that may guide parents in dealing with their children. One Sage notes that we should take a child's health into consideration when we are teaching him to fast. We are then given three different rulings about when to train a child based on the child's gender and the type of law applied (biblical edicts are more powerful than rabbinic edicts). Rabbi Yohanan appears to disagree with Rav Huna and Rav Nahman, saying that there is no rabbinic ordinance that requires minors to fast to the end of the day.

How should we teach our children to fast on Yom Kippur? We should take their health, temperament, and maturity into account and gradually introduce them to the practice. If they appear to be ready at 8 years of age to fast for a few hours, then we can encourage them to do so. If they are not capable of fasting for even a few hours until they are 10, then we wait until that time.

By the time our son was 4 years old, he knew that "we don't eat treats on Yom Kippur." He also knew that mommy and daddy were a little grouchy that day because they were hungry! [JZA, SAA]

One teaching that is implied by this passage and others, is that a child does not appear, gift-wrapped, so to speak, at his *bar mitzvah*, ready to observe Judaism. Children gradually develop their practice of Judaism over time and gradually take more and more responsibility for their Jewish lives. The *bar* or *bat mitzvah* ceremony is just one step along a road that should have seen a slow and steady increase in Jewish observance on the child's part.

Although fasting on Yom Kippur is a very important part of the holiday and it is important for us to teach children to fast, there are certain situations in which fasting is not medically appropriate. Perhaps one of the most common health questions women face in terms of their Jewish life is the question of whether to fast on Yom Kippur when they are pregnant. Our passage is part of the elaboration of the following mishnah:

> A pregnant woman who smelled [food and drink] they feed her until she recovers. (*M. Yoma* 8:5)

The Bavli explains that the woman should be fed gradually, and only just enough so that she recovers, although if she absolutely must eat pork to satisfy herself, even on Yom Kippur, she may do so (*B. Yoma* 82a). However, as we see from the following stories, it is better if she can somehow withstand the hunger.

> There was a woman with child who had smelt [a dish]. [People] came before Rabbi [questioning him what should be done]. He said to them: Go and whisper to her that it is the Day of Atonement. They whispered to her and she accepted the whispered suggestion, whereupon he [Rabbi] cited about her [the verse]: "Before I formed you in the belly I knew you" (Jeremiah 1:5). From her

came forth Rabbi Johanan. [Again] there was a woman with child who had smelt [a dish]. [People] came before Rabbi [questioning him what should be done]. He said to them: Go and whisper to her that it is the Day of Atonement. They whispered to her and she did not accept the whispered suggestion. He cited with regard to her (83a): "The wicked are estranged from the womb" (Psalm 58:4). From her came forth Shabbatia, the hoarder of provisions [for speculation]. (B. Yoma 82b–83a)

The Sages apparently felt that it was the fetus, not the mother, who developed the craving. They also seem to subscribe to the "nature over nurture" theory of personality: the child's future moral character is already formed in the womb. Sages, of course, were held in the highest esteem and those who hoarded food during famines for profit were considered the lowest of the low. So each fetus was already exhibiting its nature through the cravings of its mother. We note that it is extremely important for women who may have premature labor to be well hydrated. It is imperative in such situations that they drink adequate amounts of water, even on Yom Kippur.

> The Torah commands that on Yom Kippur we afflict our souls (Leviticus 23:27). While this is traditionally done through fasting, we can afflict ourselves spiritually when we cannot do so physically. Just making ourselves aware that we are human, that our lives are short, and that we are so greatly dependent on God's mercy should be enough to make ourselves feel afflicted when we cannot fast. [JZA, SAA]

A second situation in which the effects of fasting must be carefully considered is in adolescents with anorexia nervosa.

Dr. Tomas Silber, an adolescent medicine specialist at Children's National Medical Center in Washington, DC, has told me that he sees many Jewish girls with anorexia nervosa and one important discussion he has with them is explaining to them that they should not fast on Yom Kippur because of the potential risk to their health. In a more general sense, it is important that we teach children that fasting on Yom Kippur is not done to lose weight or make one more attractive, but rather for spiritual reasons.

Perhaps Yom Kippur is a good time to talk with your children about eating and about thinness/obesity. Certainly, if we can start sex education in elementary school, we can be open about nutrition. Eating disorders are a major crisis for our adolescents that have implications not only during childhood and adolescence, but during adulthood as well. For example, severely obese children risk adult obesity and problems with heart disease, and anorexic girls run the risk of osteoporosis in adulthood. (Adolescents and adult females with anorexia nervosa run the risk of fractures from calcium loss due both to their poor diet and decreased estrogen levels.) [SAA]

The Closeness between Children and God

Our Sages recognized that children may actually have a closer relationship with God than do adults, even though children may be unable to perform as many *mitzvot* as adults do. They also realized that children speak whatever is on their minds and that sometimes their speech may make no apparent sense at all. Instead of dismissing such children's speech, the Sages saw in it the gift of prophecy.

R. Johanan said: Since the Temple was destroyed, prophecy has been taken from prophets and given to fools and children. . . . How has prophecy been given to children? A case in point is that of the daughter of Rav Hisda. She was sitting on her father's lap, and in front of him were sitting Raba and Rami bar Hama. He said to her: Which of them would you like? She replied: Both. Whereupon Raba said: And let me be the second. (*B. Baba Batra* 12b)

Here we see a child who picks not one husband for herself, but two. We learn elsewhere (*B. Yebamot* 34b) that she married Rami bar Hama, who subsequently died, and after 10 years she married Raba. This passage is interesting, not only because it shows that the Sages, through this teaching about prophecy, give some weight to a child's words, but it also gives us a glimpse of a great rabbi sitting with his daughter in his lap and being guided by her wishes in so important a matter as who she will marry. As a child develops, we teach that child self-esteem by respecting what he does. Here, the Sages teach us to listen to our children and their preferences. The end result of believing that children are given the gift of prophecy is that we will listen more intently to our children's words. And indeed, sometimes children see and speak more clearly about issues than do adults.

How can we talk with our children about God and about the existential issues of our lives? Children ask amazingly acute questions about who made the world, where babies come from, what happens after death, and what God is like. How can we answer their questions? First, we must have thought through these issues ourselves. Our tradition provides us with many answers. For example, the Torah teaches us that God made the world by speaking. We can explain that this is one of the ways that God differs from human beings, since we cannot make something simply by saying, "Let there be X!" Second, we should feel free to make use of analogies to explain complex phenomena. Much of our relationship with God can be explained by referring to a parent–child bond. For example, to explain why God apparently does not answer prayer, we can ask a child to think about times when he's asked for something and his parents have said, "No." "No" is an answer to a request–it simply is not the desired answer. Similarly, God may not grant some of our requests, but that doesn't mean that God does not listen to our prayers. Third, we should feel free to say, "I don't know." There are some mysteries that cannot be explained, and it is fine for children to know this. Obviously, our explanations wil have to grow in sophistication as our children grow, but even adults need metaphors and analogies to talk about God.

Recently a mother brought her 5-year-old daughter to me and said, "She has a very important question to ask you."

"Does God have parents?" the girl inquired.

I laughed and said, "That's a really good question, but no, God does not have parents."

"Why not?"

"Because God is just different from us."

"Oh," she said, "okay."

The mother looked at me, astounded. "You mean, that was all I had to say? 'God is different'? I've been discussing this with her for a week!"

If you are clear about the answers in your own mind, and deliver those answers in a clear way, your kids will accept them as legitimate beliefs. The trick *is taking the time and effort to figure out what your own beliefs are.* [JZA]

The Evil Impulse and the Impulse for Good

Why do toddlers run toward the street? Why are children driven to climb up bookcases? Why, when you ask a child to give you an item, does he bring it to within three feet of you then throw it at you? Psychologists might explain these actions as expressions of curiosity or attempts by children to control their own lives. The Sages lumped curiosity, drive, ambition, competitiveness, stubbornness, and headstrong desire into one concept: *yetser hara*, the evil impulse.

The Sages recognized that we need our evil impulse. They did not want us to lock it away, or deny that it exists. All they wanted us to do is harness its energy so that we may use it productively, as we can see from the following passage.

> He [the *yetser hara*] was surrendered to them [the Sages]. . . . He [God] said to them: Realize that if you kill him, the world goes down. They imprisoned him for three days, then looked in the whole Land of Israel for a fresh egg and could not find it. Thereupon they said: What shall we do now? Shall we kill him? The world would then go down. . . . They put out his eyes and let him go. (*B. Yoma* 69b)

In this story, the evil impulse is personified and captured by the Sages. The Sages then come to realize that the world would cease to exist if we did not have the *yetser hara.* If we did not have our impulse to create, we would never have children, build buildings, and so forth. So the Sages disable the evil impulse and send him on his way. This is consistent with another of the Sages' teachings:

> Who is mighty? The one who subdues his evil impulse. (*M. Pirkei Avot* 4:1)

We do not teach our children to revile their drives and ambitions: we teach them to *control* those drives. The Sages recognized that this is terribly difficult to do; in fact, those who can control their own impulses are considered heroes.

> *This teaching, that a hero is the one who has self-control rather than the one who can hit the hardest, stands in direct contrast to what our children see on television. Yet it is this rabbinic advice that is truly practical and will help our children grow into well-adjusted members of society.*
>
> *So how do you teach children self-control when they are frustrated or angry? First, listen to their feelings and reflect them back so that they feel heard and understood. Then, channel their energy in ways that do not hurt themselves or others. If they must hit something, let them hit a pillow, or give "time out" to whatever is making them angry. For example, let's say the child is working on a math problem and is frustrated. Let the child give the book "time out" and then help the child to get back on task. If he is angry with another person, help your child to understand his own feelings and then try to explain the other person's point of view.* [SAA, JZA]

When do we acquire our evil impulse? The Sages believe that we acquire it when we are born.

> Antoninus asked Rabbi, "At what time does the impulse to evil gain mastery over a person—at the time of his conception or at the time he is born?" Rabbi: "At the time of his conception." Antoninus: "If so, he would have kicked his way out of his mother's womb. Accordingly, the impulse to evil must gain mastery at the time of birth." (B. Sanhedrin 91b)

We are born with curiosity about our world and a wish to explore it and master it. We are born with needs and desires, and from our first moments we strive to have those needs and desires taken care of. Even the tiniest infant soon learns that crying brings milk, comfort, a new diaper, and so forth. Or, for another example, anyone who has watched an infant determinedly rock on its hands and knees in preparation for crawling, or watched him try time and again to pull to a standing position only to land— hard!—will recognize that our drive to explore and master space is something inborn rather than taught. It is this drive and determination that the Sages wish we would harness for holy purposes.

Protecting Our Children from Danger

We cannot depend on young children to control their "evil inclinations." A young child's curiosity about his environment will lead him to danger if that environment has not been made safe.

When an infant lies in his cot and places his hand upon a snake or a scorpion so that he is bitten, this was caused by none other than the evil inclination which is in his body. Or when he lays his hand on glowing coals and is burnt, this was caused by none other than the evil inclination which is within his body since the evil inclination it is that drives him headlong [to destruction]. Observe, however, a kid or lamb: when it sees a well it turns back, since there is no evil inclination in a beast [to lead it to harm]. (*Avot d'Rabbi Natan* 16:3)

A young child is curious about everything. Accordingly, it is a parent's responsibility to make a child's environment as safe as possible. Even the most innocuous things can be dangerous to an exploring child. For example, many traditional families who do not cook on the Sabbath use a hot plate that is kept warm. Unfortunately, it is a source of danger itself. One study in Israel documented severe burns in some toddlers who had, out of curiosity, played with Sabbath hot plates. Some of these burns were severe enough to need reconstructive surgery.[4]

No one could complete a pediatric residency without having the experience of caring for a child who has been a drowning or near-drowning victim. These accidents are just as likely to occur in bath tubs as in swimming pools. I remember several such bath tub tragedies, and when our children were born I made a rule that "we don't leave the kids in the tub by themselves no matter what." Phone callers can call back (or you can bring your cordless phone in the bathroom during bathtime). It literally takes only seconds for an infant to drown. [SAA]

When can we rely on a child not to lead himself into danger because of curiosity? The Sages rule that when a child reaches his majority (12 for girls, 13 for boys) we can trust a child's conscience to tell it to stop when it is tempted to pursue a self-destructive course of action.

> The impulse to evil is thirteen years older than the impulse to good. It begins growing with a child in the mother's womb and comes out with him. If the child is about to profane the Sabbath, it does not deter him; if the child is about to take a life, it does not deter him; if the child is about to commit an act of unchastity, it does not deter him. At the age of thirteen the impulse to good is born in a child. If then he is about to profane the Sabbath, it warns him: "You fool! Scripture states, 'Everyone that profanes it [the Sabbath] shall surely be put to death'" (Exodus 31:14). If he is about to take a life, it warns him, "You fool! Scripture says, 'Whoso sheds blood, by man shall his blood be shed'" (Genesis 9:6). If he is about to commit an act of unchastity, it warns him: "You fool! Scripture states, 'Both the adulterer and the adulteress shall surely be put to death'" (Leviticus 20:10). (*Avot d'Rabbi Natan* 16:2)

As we see from these passages, the Sages felt that we are born with our evil impulse, our drives and appetites, and only acquire our impulse to do good, that is, our conscience, when we go through puberty. Learning to tame the animal part of our nature is a gradual process that can only be fully accomplished by mature persons. Therefore, the Sages considered parents responsible for their child's actions until the child reached the age of majority. After that, the Sages considered the child to be responsible for his own actions.

Of course, a child's conscience can only warn him if he's been taught the texts and lessons that form the basis of moral knowledge. If we do our jobs as parents and inculcate these values through setting limits and teaching lessons in the first 13 years of the child's life, then the Sages are telling us that those lessons will have "taken."

How much freedom and responsibility should we give a 13-year-old child? This is difficult to answer. Increasingly, younger children are being left home or given responsibilities for which they are unprepared. If we are going to leave teenagers by themselves, they ought to know basic first aid, including cardiopulmonary resuscitation, and be able to handle emergencies such as fires, power outages, and the like. [JZA, SAA]

Education for Gifted Children: Accelerating Children's Progress

We all have our favorite stories about children doing precocious things or pronouncing clever witticisms. Rabbinic literature contains many such stories about schoolchildren, particularly about Sages as schoolchildren. For example, we learn that schoolchildren, then as now, make the challenge of learning the Hebrew alphabet into a game.

There is the following story: On a cloudy day, on which Sages did not come to the meeting house, the children came in and said, "Let us hold a session, so that the study time will not be lost." They said, what is that which is written: [Two kinds of] *mem, nun, tsadi, pey, caf*? It means, "From saying [of the Lord] to saying, from Faithful to faithful, from the Righteous one to the righteous, from the

Mouth to the mouth, from the Palm of the Holy One, blessed be He, to the palm of the hand of Moses." (*Y. Megillah* 1:9, 71d)

This passage illustrates how some children love learning about their Judaism, particularly about the Hebrew alphabet. One of the most difficult things to learn about this is which letters take final forms. These children chose words beginning with each letter having a final form (i.e., *mem*, *nun*, *tsadi*, *pey*, and *caf*), each word emphasizing the concept of a reliable tradition passed down through the generations. For the letter *mem*, the two forms of the letter stand for the transmission from one saying to another saying (*mima'amar l'ma'amar*). The two forms of the letter *nun* stand for transmission from one faithful one to another faithful one (in Hebrew: *mine'eman l'ne'eman*). The two forms of the letter *tsadi* represent the transmission from righteous one to righteous one (in Hebrew: *mitsadik l'tsadik*). The two forms of the letter *pey* stand for the transmission from one mouth to another mouth (in Hebrew: *mi peh l'peh*). And the two forms of the letter *caf* reminded them of the transmission of the Torah from the palm of the hand of the Holy One, blessed be He, to the palm of the hand of Moses (in Hebrew: *micaf shel HaKadosh Baruch Hu el caf Moshe*). In other words, in these letters the children see hints regarding the continuous process of passing on the revelation received at Sinai, one commandment at a time, from one righteous, faithful person to another, throughout the generations. The children were able to learn not only the forms of the alphabet, but the essence of tradition, as well. These children were obviously motivated to study Hebrew, and we would expect that their parents encouraged them.

This passage reflects a basic truth: some children, in fact most children, like learning Hebrew. It's a skill they know they'll use and their progress is quantifiable: they can read something this week that they couldn't read last week. Certainly, we want to ecourage our children to enjoy learning Hebrew, as the children in this passage did. However, even our zeal for Hebrew learning has to have balance to it. Some bar mitzvah students come to their studies with a fear of making mistakes that borders on phobia. As I explain to every one of them, the point of leading the service is to take on an adult role in the congregation, not to turn in a mistake-free "performance," because everyone makes mistakes. You must feel good about yourself and what you're doing and know that the people who love you love you even if you make mistakes. [JZA]

Can children move more swiftly through a curriculum if they have special intellectual or spiritual gifts? The Sages would answer, yes. For example, they allow a child who has not yet reached the age of majority to participate in certain rituals if the child understands the nature of the ritual and knows to whom prayer is addressed.

A boy [younger than 13 years old] who knows to whom the benediction is addressed (i.e., God) may be counted for *zimmun* [the invitation to say grace after meals]. Abaye and Rava [when they were boys] were once sitting before Rabbah. Said Rabbah to them, "To whom do we address the benedictions?"

They replied, "To the All Merciful."

"And where does the All Merciful abide?" Rava pointed to the roof; Abaye went outside and pointed to the sky.

Said Rabbah to them, "Both of you will become Rabbis." (*B. Berachot* 48a)

Zimmun is the invitation to say the grace after meals (not to be confused with the actual grace after meals). It may only be recited if three adult persons (either three women alone, or three men) are present. In this passage, the Sages recognize that if a child understands what the ritual is about, he is not to be disqualified because of his age: he may be included among the three persons who are needed to say the *zimmun*. In a sense, then, this child would have advanced through the curriculum of his Jewish studies.

> *Just as some children have more talent for playing baseball or the piano than other children, some children will be more interested in Judaism and spirituality than other children. And just as we would foster a talent for piano playing by providing lessons and encouraging practice, so we can foster a spiritual nature in children by providing them with opportunities to worship and by explaining their tradition to them. Similarly, learning to read music is a skill that could serve almost all children well, even if they are not destined to be Isaac Stern. So, too, teaching a child about Judaism is appropriate even if he doesn't show signs of being the next Maimonides.*
>
> *And how do parents decide between, let's say, soccer practice and Hebrew school? One parent I know said it best when she commented, "The chances that he'll be a professional soccer player are almost nil, but he'll be a Jew his whole life long."* [JZA]

The Sages readily admit that they can be outwitted by children and women: wisdom and sharpness are not the exclusive preserve of grown males.

Rabbi Joshua ben Hananiah remarked: No one has ever had the better of me except a woman, a little boy and a little girl. What was the incident with the woman? I was once staying at an inn where the hostess served me with beans. On the first day I ate all of them leaving nothing. On the second day, too, I left nothing. On the third day she over-seasoned them with salt, and, as soon as I tasted them, I withdrew my hand. She said to me, "Rabbi, why do you not eat?" I said to her, "I have already eaten earlier in the day." She said to me, "Then you should have withdrawn your hand from the bread." She [then] said to me, "My Master, is it possible that you left [the dish today] as compensation for the former meals, for have not the Sages laid down: Nothing is to be left in the pot but something must be left in the plate?" (*Derech Eretz Rabbah* 6:3).

What was the incident with the little girl? I was walking on the road and it crossed a field and I walked on it. One girl [then] said to me, "Rabbi, is this not a field?" I said to her, "No, it is a trodden road." She said to me, "Robbers like yourself have trodden it down."

What was the incident with the little boy? I was walking on the road when I saw a little boy sitting at a cross-road. I said to him, "By what road do we go to the town?" He said to me, "This one is short but long and that one is long but short." I proceeded along the "short but long" road. When I approached the town I discovered that it was hedged in by gardens and orchards. Turning back I said to him, "My son, did you not tell me that this road was short?" He said to me, "And did I not also tell you: But long?" I kissed him upon his head and said to him, "Happy are you, O Israel, all of you are wise, both young and old." (*B. Eruvin* 53b)

In this three-part story, we learn how a great Sage could be outwitted. We should note that Rabbi Joshua ben

Hananiah was one of the kindest, gentlest, smartest, and financially poorest of the Sages. He was greatly beloved for his wisdom and his humility. It is consistent with his character that he would tell such stories about himself—jokes at his own expense. It may also be a mark of the confidence he had in his own intellect and of his self-esteem that he could tell these stories.

In the first story, he is caught in a potentially embarrassing situation. On two previous nights he cleaned his plate, but on the third night, he cannot eat the food. He tries to excuse his lack of appetite by saying that he had already eaten. But the cook notes that the rabbi did eat bread, meaning that he is hungry and is therefore not exactly telling the truth. Then the cook lets him off the hook, so to speak, by attributing his behavior to a fine rule of etiquette. Notice that it is the woman who remembers the rule and the Sage who forgets to quote it.

The incident with the girl involves the sort of behavior that violates the law but that is generally practiced anyway (something akin to jaywalking). Although everyone does it, it is still incorrect. Rabbi Joshua was walking on a path through a field. Naturally, the farmer would rather that this area be land on which he could grow crops rather than a path. However, once it had been trampled down, people continued to use the trampled area as a path, perhaps thinking the farmer had permitted its presence. The little girl rebukes the Sage for continuing to ruin the field. He replies that it is permissible for him to walk there since it is already trampled down. Whereupon, she notes that people such as he are really robbing the farmer of some of his land, and Rabbi Joshua has to tacitly admit that she is right.

Finally, the little boy, speaking in riddles, outwits the

Sage. The route that appears to be a shortcut will not lead into the town and is the "short but long way." The way that appears to be longer is actually shorter because one does not have to double back: it does lead into the town. It is characteristic of Rabbi Joshua ben Hananiah that instead of being irritated, he rejoices at the boy's cleverness and praises him.

From these passages, we learn that the Sages valued intellectual and spiritual sharpness in boys and girls, men and women. They did not feel competitive with these children or insecure around them. Rather, Rabbi Joshua may serve as our role model: he praises children's accomplishments and so reinforces them.

A constant theme in rabbinic literature is that Torah knowledge and virtue transcend gender and age. In other words, the Sages valued these qualities no matter where they found them. Passing this value system on to our children will help them value people for their true, inner worth and understand others better. [SAA, JZA]

Parental Involvement with a Child's Education

For the Sages, intellectual activity (i.e., studying Jewish texts) was also a spiritual pursuit. They did not bifurcate the intellectual and spiritual realms. Theirs was a holistic view of development. The Sages felt that a child's spiritual and intellectual development was something that a parent should properly oversee. (It is not in our day alone that parents devote their evening hours to doing homework and their morning hours to seeing their children off to school.) Parents were involved in their children's education from the beginning of their lives in the rabbinic era. For example, Rabbi Joshua ben Hananiah's greatness is attributed to his mother's diligence in bringing him to the synagogue from the earliest age:

> He [R. Dosa b. Harkinas] saw Rabbi Joshua and recited in his regard [the following verse]: "Whom will he teach knowledge, and to whom will he explain the message? Those who are weaned from the milk and those taken from the breast" (Isaiah 28:9). I remember that his mother would bring his cradle to the synagogue, so that his ears should cleave to the teachings of the Torah. (*Y. Yebamot* 1:6, 3a)

Rabbi Dosa ben Harkinas attributes Rabbi Joshua's greatness to his early exposure to Jewish teaching. Rabbi Joshua's mother was obviously well motivated to make her son a Sage and put forth early and constant effort to see that he became one.

The verse from Isaiah quoted in this passage is, in itself, a model for how to teach young children. In it, God despairs of teaching the adult Israelites who have gone far away from their faith. Therefore, God decides to teach the youngest children. The verse that follows the one quoted above (Isaiah 28:9) hints at the way one teaches young children: with repetition, with patience, and with word games, which must be heard in Hebrew to be appreciated:

> Therefore [will God teach these young children] *tsav l'tsav tsav l'tsav, kav l'kav kav l'kav; z'eir sham z'eir sham*; a precept upon precept, precept upon precept; line

upon line, line upon line; here a little and there a little. (Isaiah 28:10)

In this verse (Isaiah 28:10) there is obvious wordplay and rhyming that describe the process of learning. It illustrates how learning is accomplished: bit by bit, from one's youth, and with a sense of fun, too.

How often have I heard parents, particularly intermarried parents, say, "We'll wait until our children reach their teens and let them pick their own religion." Waiting until the teen years is far too late. As parents, we have an obligation to give our children a way of understanding the world and the role they are to play in it. This is properly done through religious education. The sooner a child's religious education is begun, the better. Putting off educating a child in his or her faith simply hurts the child. And the child, in general, will not allow it. The child will end up asking, "What am I? What is Daddy? What is Mommy?" It is best to have ready straightforward answers to such questions, providing them before being asked, if possible. [JZA]

Seeing to a child's education was considered more important than personal dignity to at least one Sage:

Rabbi Hiyya bar Abba found Rabbi Joshua ben Levi wearing a plain cloth upon his head [instead of more appropriate headgear] and taking a child to the synagogue [for study]. "What is the meaning of all this?" he demanded. He [Rabbi Joshua] said to him, "Is it then a small thing that it is written, 'And you shall make them known to your sons and your sons' sons' (Deuteronomy 4:9); which is followed by 'That is the day that you stood before the Lord your God in Horeb'" (Deuteronomy 4:10). From then onwards Rabbi Hiyya bar Abba did not taste meat [i.e., eat breakfast] before reviewing [the previous day's lesson] with the child and adding [another verse]. (*B. Kiddushin* 30a)

This is a picture most parents can identify with. There is Rabbi Joshua ben Levi flying out of the house to take his son to school without getting his tie tied, his cuffs buttoned, or his shoe laces tied, as it were. (What Rabbi Joshua was doing was apparently much like people in synagogue today who, unable to find a *kippah*, put a napkin on their heads: it isn't exactly appropriate, but it does serve its purpose.) When his colleague questions him, Rabbi Joshua replies, basically, that he has his priorities straight: getting his son to school on time is more important than immaculate grooming. The two verses that he uses to justify his position are juxtaposed in the Torah, and the Sages considered these juxtapositions important. So, they reasoned, if a verse about teaching your children is placed next to a verse about standing before God at Mount Sinai (Horeb is another name for Mount Sinai), then it means that teaching your children is equivalent to standing at Mount Sinai when the Law was given. Rabbi Joshua's statement appears to have convinced Rabbi Hiyya bar Abba, for he thereafter follows Rabbi Joshua's lead: he starts his day by helping his son with his homework and giving him a jump on the day's new lessons.

In the Jewish community, religious school teachers are often faced with parents who claim their children are not learning anything in the 2 hours a week they spend on religious studies. The teachers counter that they are frustrated by trying to teach practices and beliefs that the children do not experience at home. The obvious solution is for parents to be as involved with their children's Jewish education as with their secular education. We can enrich children's Jewish education in many ways: by practicing Judaism at home, by participating in synagogue services and programs, and by sending them to Jewish day schools, if available, as well as to Jewish summer camps and to Israel. [JZA, SAA]

Parents' concerns with the Jewish education the community provides are not new. Indeed, we learn of educational reforms in the days of the Sages that could well be implemented today. A man named Joshua ben Gamala saw that the only children receiving an education were the ones being educated by their own fathers. Therefore he instituted a system whereby teachers were assigned to each town and the children's education was publicly provided starting at the age of 6 or 7 (*B. Baba Batra* 21a). The student–teacher ratio and the quality of a child's teacher were as crucial to his education then as they are today. In addition, the Sages recognized that some teachers are better than others when they instituted the following rules:

Raba further said: The number of pupils to be assigned to each teacher is twenty-five. If there are fifty, we appoint two teachers. If there are forty, we appoint an assistant at the expense of the town.

Raba also said: If we have a teacher who gets on with the children and there is another who can get on better, we do not replace the first by the second, for fear that the second when appointed will become indolent. Rav Dimi from Nehardea, however, held that he would exert himself still more if appointed. . . .

Raba further said: If there are two teachers of whom one gets on fast but with mistakes and the other slowly but without mistakes, we appoint the one who gets on fast and makes mistakes, since the mistakes correct themselves in time. Rav Dimi from Nehardea on the other hand said that we appoint the one who goes slowly but makes no mistakes, for once a mistake is implanted it cannot be eradicated. (*B. Baba Batra* 21a)

These rules presuppose a great deal of parental involvement in a child's schooling: we are supposed to be involved in maintaining a good student–teacher ratio in our child's class and in making sure that inadequate teachers are replaced. There is a difference of opinion between Raba and Rav Dimi about whether teachers should be replaced. Raba feels they should not be replaced, since the new teacher might become self-satisfied and lazy, while Rav Dimi assumes that the newly appointed teacher will be energized and work diligently. No "bottom line" is prescribed and, obviously, conflicts with teachers and schools should be worked out on a case-by-case basis. Raba and Rav Dimi further dispute who is the better teacher: one who is quick but inaccurate or one who teaches slowly and accurately. Generally, the opinion cited last in a Talmudic passage is the opinion that is more authoritative. However, an actual decision about a teacher must be based on the nature of the subject and the class of students being taught.

How do you deal with a religious school teacher about whom your child complains? First, sitting in the class to observe, which can usually be easily arranged through the principal of the school, will help you assess the situation from an adult perspective. Most

*religious school teachers are well meaning and under-
paid and could benefit from parental support. You
could offer to help in the classroom or become a religious school teacher yourself. Of course, if the teacher
cannot or will not benefit from additional training
and/or feedback, then he may have to be dismissed,
but that's obviously the last resort.* [SAA, JZA]

While a teacher can teach many subjects, there are
some things that children best learn from their parents.
For example, we learn that parents are responsible not
only for leading a Passover seder, but also for making it
a pleasant experience.

It was related of Rabbi Akiba that he used to distribute
parched ears and nuts on the eve of Passover, so that the
children might not fall asleep but ask [questions].
  It was taught, Rabbi Eliezer said: The *matzot* are eaten
hastily on the night of Passover, on account of the children, so that they should not fall asleep. . . .
  Our Rabbis taught: A person is in duty bound to make
his children and the members of his household rejoice on
a festival. (*B. Pesachim* 109a–b)

Rabbi Akiba and Rabbi Eliezer are both concerned that
the children at a seder be able to stay awake to enjoy the
evening's rituals and to ask questions, since children and
their questions are the focus of the seder. We note that
these great Sages, themselves, take care that the children
will be alert while the story of the Exodus is told and the
Passover symbols are explained.

*The Sages were obviously aware that a parent's whis-
per carries more weight than a teacher's shout. Chil-*

dren will emulate their parents, and if the parents value Judaism, know about Judaism, and take the time to teach their children about Judaism, the children will learn to love their Judaism. [JZA, SAA]

Today, parents who personally communicate their beliefs to their children about the use of drugs, about sex, about violence in relationships, and about maintaining personal safety and self-respect are simply following the example of the Sages who were also involved in teaching their children about life. While these issues certainly have medical aspects to them, they can also be looked at as religious issues. If parents remind their children that they are created in God's image and that they are supremely loved and worthy of respect, they will be teaching them lessons from the Jewish religion. (How do we talk about God's image to our children? We can begin by asking them to recall a time they felt great joy or were overwhelmed by the beauty of nature or felt well and truly loved. Those feelings are a glimpse of God's image.) Instilling self-esteem in our children may be one of the most effective forms of "preventive medicine" for times when children have to make choices about sex, drugs, relationships, and safety.

Teaching Charity to Children

"I don't want to share!" How many times have parents heard this battle cry from their children? Teaching children to share is one of the most difficult things a parent must do. However, the rewards of teaching children kindness last a lifetime. The Sages categorized generosity in two main ways: *tsedakah* (monetary generosity) and *gemilut hasadim* (deeds of loving kindness). Donating blankets to a shelter for the homeless or money to a synagogue would be examples of *tsedakah*, while visiting someone who is sick or helping prepare a person for burial are examples of *gemilut hasadim. Tsedakah* and *gemilut hasadim* are highly valued in Judaism, not only because they bring the obvious benefits to a community, but because they offer the donor eternal rewards.

> Rabbi Eleazar stated, Greater is he who performs *tsedakah* than [he who offers] all the sacrifices. . . . Our Rabbis taught, in three respects is *gemilut hasadim* superior to *tsedakah*: *tsedakah* can be done [only] with one's money, but *gemilut hasadim* can be done with one's person and one's money. *Tsedakah* can be given [only] to poor persons, *gemilut hasadim* both to poor persons and rich persons. *Tsedakah* can be given to the living only, *gemilut hasadim* can be done both to the living and to the dead. And Rabbi Eleazar said, He who executes charity and justice is regarded as though he had filled all the world with kindness. (*B. Sukkah* 49b)

The Sages encourage us to view *tsedakah* as a replacement for, and improvement on, the sacrifices as a means of personal redemption. The sacrifices that were offered in the Temple were, in part, the way people atoned for their sins and gave themselves a fresh start. Today, when we are feeling bad about ourselves, we can give *tsedakah* or do acts of loving kindness as a way of restoring our self-esteem.

Though only some persons need *tsedakah*, everyone needs to be shown kindness and consideration. Teaching children to think of others and give of themselves may simply be a matter of raising the issue consistently. A recent study examined how Jewish children learned to give charity. The authors found that the adolescents gave less charity than younger children. On interviewing teachers, however, the authors found that there was a lower expectation of charity-giving by adolescents. The suggestion was that because we assume teens are self-centered and rebellious, they behave that way.[5]

> *Honesty and charity are learned characteristics. If we make fun of the homeless, laugh about "bellringers" and door-to-door collections for disease research and prevention, then our children will follow suit. Likewise, if we put our loose change in* pushkes *and practice other forms of* tsedakah *and* gemilut hasadim, *our children will, in all likelihood, take the example to heart.* [SAA, JZA]

Learning Styles and Learning Disabilities

As parents, we want our children to succeed academically. The Sages were aware of the characteristics that make for more effective and less effective students. For example, they broke down the traits of a good student into seven characteristics:

> [There are] seven things in a stupid person and seven in a wise person: a wise man does not speak before one who is greater than he in wisdom, and does not interrupt his fellow's words, and is not hasty to answer; he asks in accordance with the subject-matter, and he answers in accordance with the accepted decision; and he speaks of the first [point] first, and of the last [point] last; and

concerning that which he has not heard, he says: I have
not heard; and he acknowledges the truth. And the re-
verse of these [are characteristic] in a stupid person. (*M.
Pirkei Avot* 5:9)

A good student, according to the Sages, listens well, does
not interrupt, thinks before offering an answer, does not
wander off the topic, answers from a base of knowledge
that is generally accepted, thinks in an orderly fashion,
and knows the limits of his knowledge. A poor student,
by implication, would not listen well, would interrupt,
would answer questions impulsively, would not stay on
task, would answer questions nonsensically, would exhibit
disorganized thinking, and would not be able to recognize
the limits of his own knowledge. These traits are still important for effective learning.

The Sages also recognized that people have different
capabilities to learn and different styles of learning:

Even so does a fool say: "Who can learn the whole of the
Torah? [The first three tractates of] *Nezikin* [i.e., *Baba
Kamma*, *Baba Metsia*, and *Baba Batra*] contain thirty
chapters, [the tractates related to] *Keilim* has thirty chapters? [There is too much material there to learn!]," while
the sensible person says: "I shall learn two small sections
today and two small sections tomorrow, until I shall have
learnt the whole Torah." . . . So too does the fool say:
"What good will I do by learning Torah and forgetting it?"
whereas the sensible man says: "Does not the Holy One,
blessed be He, give reward for the very labor [of Torah
study]?" (*Leviticus Rabbah*, *Metsorah* 19:2)

Here, another characteristic of a successful learner is
described: the ability to break down a very large task into

small sections that can be easily accomplished. Instead of looking at the sum total of what must be learned and giving up before beginning, the Sages urge us to take a slow but steady approach to attaining the goal of Torah study and, by implication, secular study as well.

Learning Torah is somewhat different from learning in the secular sphere. We learn to count so that we can balance our checkbooks. There is no special merit to learning math beyond its practical benefits. When we learn Torah, however, we earn a reward, whether conceptualized as a reward from God or the reward of feeling connected to a beautiful and meaningful tradition that is our own. The reward is contingent on the learning, even if we forget what we have learned and have to relearn it. In other words, one need not be a brilliant scholar to study Torah and rabbinic literature. What is more important is the constancy with which the study is accomplished. Rabbinic literature is so vast that it cannot be mastered like other, more finite bodies of knowledge. There is no finish line with Torah study; no end of the semester, no final grade. It differs from secular knowledge in that we can, and should, always be acquiring it, and in that as long as we are engaged in the process, we are succeeding.

That said, we must admit that Torah study is easier for some and harder for others. Some students have to put forth great effort to learn even a small amount of material. One example of a student with such a learning disability, and the right way to deal with such a student, are described in this passage:

> Rabbi P'rida had a pupil whom he taught his lesson four hundred times before the latter could master it. One day it was requested that he participate in a *mitzvah* [after

he taught this student]. He taught him [in the usual man-
ner] but he could not grasp the lesson. He [Rabbi P'rida]
said to him, "What is the matter today?" The student said
to him, "From the moment the Master was told that there
was a religious matter to be attended to I could not concentrate my thoughts, for at every moment I imagined,
now the Master will get up or now the Master will get up."
He [Rabbi P'rida] said to him, "Give me your attention
and I will teach you again", and so he taught him another
four hundred times. A *Bat Kol* [a Heavenly Voice] issued
forth asking him, "Do you prefer that four hundred years
shall be added to your life or that you and your generation shall be privileged to have a share in the world to
come?" He said, "That I and my generation shall be privileged to have a share in the world to come." The Holy
One blessed be He said, "Give him both that [reward] and
the other [reward]." (*B. Eruvin* 54b)

This passage can be seen as an ancient commentary on
a condition we now refer to as "attention deficit disorder."
It appears that the pupil in the story had trouble focusing
on his lesson. The teacher gets his pupil's attention and
then proceeds to repeat the lesson until it is learned. For
this patience the teacher is rewarded by God.

*Most synagogues will go out of their way to make
arrangements for a child with learning disabilities to
have a religious education. They can adapt the requirements for a bar or bat mitzvah to your child's abilities.
However, and this is a big however, a synagogue cannot be sensitive if you do not let them know what is
going on. I would encourage parents of children with
learning or mental disabilities to talk over their child's
situation with their rabbi or religious educator who*

will, in almost all cases, be sensitive and adaptable.
[JZA]

Attention deficit disorder is a common problem in which children, and adults, may have difficulty focusing on specific tasks, such as their studies. There is intense, ongoing research into its cause and treatment. Individual instruction and frequent repetition are educational methods that may help such students. Teachers and parents with the patience for these methods deserve to be rewarded.

Families should consult an appropriate expert in the field, such as a child psychiatrist or pediatrician, in evaluating what is best for their child. I am personally aware of numerous children who have been aided by judicious use of medications that help them maintain their attention. The use of medication for this condition, as with the use of any medication, has its potential risks and benefits and should be carefully considered on an individual basis. [SAA]

Concluding Thoughts on Child Development

Rabbinic literature teaches us what we probably already know. The more we value our Judaism and take personal responsibility for transmitting it, the more likely it is that our children will value Judaism. The Sages also reinforce what every good teacher practices: we should talk to our children in ways that are appropriate for their particular stage of cognitive and spiritual development. As our children grow, so should our explanations of Judaism grow in sophistication. Of course, this demands constant learning on our own part. In this way, our children can actually help us be more dedicated to learning about Judaism.

8

Parent–Child Relationships: Then and Now

As new parents quickly learn, family dynamics are altered forever when a baby arrives. The bond between parents and their children begins even before the moment of birth. As this relationship grows and becomes more complex, we need additional skills to deal with our children and with our changing relationship with our spouse. After all, before having children we rented the videotapes we wanted to see instead of endlessly watching "Sesame Street" or "Willy Wonka."

Although this may destroy our credibility with some readers, we must confess up front that we allow our children to watch "Barney and Friends." The kids adore it and we tolerate it. Admittedly, it doesn't have the clever scripts and universal appeal of "Sesame Street" (who could beat Danny DeVito and Rhea Pearlman singing "Rubber Duckie"?), but it teaches the kids valuable lessons about friendship and safety. Most importantly, they like it. We don't expect them to like all of our shows, so why can't they have a show that only they like? Besides, it's great fun thinking up variant versions of the Barney song. [JZA, SAA]

We were more likely to be connoisseurs of restaurants than of parks and their playground equipment. And of course, now we must learn to juggle the needs of all our different family members, spending more time ferrying children to different activities than we imagined possible. In this chapter, we will examine how parents and children relate to each other beginning with birth, and how that relationship changes as our children grow.

New children affect our pets, too. When we brought our second child home, our dog was so scared that he ran, shaking, into our bedroom and hid. You could almost hear him thinking, "What strange torture are they inflicting on me now?" He soon learned that a baby is a great source of spilled food, but that first day he was petrified. [SAA, JZA]

The Bond between Parent and Child

When does a child's attachment to her parents, particularly her mother, begin? In the following passage, we learn that the Sages conduct an experiment to determine the answer to that question:

A [divorced woman] once came before Samuel [declaring her refusal to nurse her son]. He said to Rav Dimi bar Joseph, "Go and test her case [to see if the child recognizes his mother]." He went and placed her among a row of women and, taking hold of her child, carried him in front of them. When he came up to her [the child] looked at her face, but she turned her eye away from him. He said to her, "Lift up your eyes, come, take away your son." How does a blind child know [its mother]? Rav Ashi said: By the smell and the taste [of the milk]. (B. *Ketubot* 60a)

This passage is part of a discussion of a mother's obligations to nurse her infant. This divorced woman did not want to nurse her child, but the Sages held that if the child recognized his mother, she is made to nurse him and paid a wage to do so. (She must nurse him because they believed he would not nurse from any other woman and would therefore die if his mother would not nurse him.)

This passage suggests that the Sages were aware of the bonding relationship between an infant and her mother or whoever nurses her. Considerable research has examined the development of an infant's ability to recognize her mother. The statements in this passage are very much in line with the views of some contemporary researchers who have suggested that even in the first week of life infants recognize their mothers by sight and smell.[1]

There is controversy over the importance of bonding in the first hours of life. Some research studies have suggested this is very important to developing the mother–child bond. However, many authors have sharply criticized this view. They emphasize that although bonding in the first hours of life is important, parents who must be separated from their newborn (e.g., in the case of a newborn who is ill or premature) should not feel guilty or expect that their child will never properly bond with them.[2]

There are many ways to bond with one's premature infant. One method, which has only recently gained some acceptance in the United States, is called "skin to skin" contact, or "kangaroo" care. This means taking a premature infant (as small as 2 or 3 pounds) out of the incubator and holding her up against her mother's or father's skin for up to an hour or more. Preliminary studies suggest that the preemies respond by improving their breathing patterns and have no trouble staying warm. Of course, it's great for the parents, too.

For full-term infants, I strongly encourage parents to have 24-hour rooming-in when allowed and feasible. This leads to more natural and more frequent nursing with lowered levels of jaundice in some infants. (Jaundice can be worsened by infrequent feeding in the first few days of life. Feeding on demand has been shown to decrease its severity.) Of course, nowadays many infants go home within 24 hours of birth anyway due to insurance rules—kind of an enforced 24-hour rooming-in plan. [SAA]

The Sages tell many stories that testify to the power of the parent–child bond, often using the example of Dama ben Netinah, a non-Jew, who honored his mother even when she did not honor him.

When Rav Dimi came, he said: He [Dama son of Netinah] was once wearing a gold embroidered silken cloak and sitting among the great men of Rome, when his mother came, tore it off from him, struck him on the head and spat in his face, yet he did not shame her.

Abimi, son of Rabbi Abbahu, recited: One may give his father pheasants as food, yet [this] drives him from the world; whereas another may make him grind in a mill and [this brings him] to the world to come.

Rabbi Abbahu said, My son Abimi has fulfilled the precept of honoring [one's parents]. Abimi had five ordained sons in his father's lifetime, yet when Rabbi Abbahu came and called out at the door, he himself speedily went and opened it for him, crying, "Yes, yes" until he reached it. One day he said to him, "Give me a drink of water." By the time he brought it he had fallen asleep. Then he bent and stood over him until he awoke. (*B. Kiddushin* 31a–b)

We will explain the first and last examples in this passage before we expand on the themes of the middle paragraph. Dama ben Netinah was obviously a well-to-do fellow whose polished image was ruined by his mother's rudeness. Yet he did not shame her or rebuke her but accepted this behavior.

What are a child's obligations to a parent who is behaving irrationally? This question arises for children when their parents abuse chemical substances or behave in abusive ways. This question also arises for adult children of parents who have lost their mental capacities. In all such cases, we must weigh the needs of all concerned and be sure that the least damage is done to each person's integrity while making sure that young children and older parents who are irrational are out of harm's way. [JZA, SAA]

Abimi's behavior with his father (outlined in the third paragraph) testifies to a common phenomenon: no matter how successful we may become in our professional and personal lives, we are still merely our parents' children when we are with our parents. In Abimi's case, even though he was a Sage and he had raised five sons to be Sages, he would wait on his father solicitously. When his father was at the door, Abimi would continue to shout "Yes, yes!" so that his father would know that he was quickly running to open the door. In the instance when his father fell asleep, Abimi hovered near until he had completed fulfilling his father's request.

Abimi's teaching about the two sons (outlined in the second paragraph) alludes to a passage found more fully in the Yerushalmi:

> How could one feed his father pheasants yet receive *Gehenna* as his inheritance? A person used to feed his father pheasants. One time [fearing that his son might have misappropriated birds set aside for sacrificial use] his father said to him, "Son, where did you get these [fine birds]?" [His son] said to him, "Old man, old man! Eat and don't complain [about the food], just like dogs that eat [whatever is before them] and don't complain!" Such a person turns out to feed his father pheasants, yet he receives Gehenna as his inheritance.
>
> How could one who yokes his father to the millstones receive the Garden of Eden as his inheritance? A person was grinding at the millstones. When the command came [for one member of each household] to grind [at the royal mill, in service of the king, the son] said to [his father], "Father, you take up the yoke here in my place, [and I shall go take up the more severe work of grinding for the king]. [In this way,] should we [at the royal mill] come to dishonor, it will be better for me—me and not you—[to be dishonored]; should we [at the royal mill] receive lashes,

it will be better for me—me and not you—[to receive them]."
[Such a person] turns out to yoke his father to the mill-
stones yet receive the Garden of Eden as his inheritance.
(*Y. Peah* 1:1, 15c)

In this passage's first case, the son feeds his father lav-
ishly but through immoral behavior, that is, stealing. (We
might conjecture from this story that the father and son
are not well-to-do and could not legitimately afford such
fancy food and this is why the father is suspicious in the
first place.) When the father questions his son, he is told
to shut up and eat, as dogs do. Thus, even though the
son is providing for his father, he is not behaving in a way
consistent with his father's values, and therefore merits
punishment in Gehenna. On the other hand, if a father
and son must both do hard labor, but the son acts out of
consideration for his father and consistent with the values his father has taught him, then he honors his father
even if he has him doing hard labor.

> *Even a young child will understand some of these con-
> cepts. Children know that if their mother asks them to
> give her an item, and instead they drop it on purpose
> or throw it at her, that this is not exactly what their
> mother had in mind. They can also be taught to frame
> kindness and politeness as "doing mitzvot." [SAA, JZA]*

Discipline

The problem of what to do with a rebellious, uncoopera-
tive child has plagued parents for centuries. Certainly, our
earliest Jewish source, the Torah, gives us one way of
handling this problem.

> If a man has a stubborn and rebellious son, that will not hearken to the voice of his father, or the voice of his mother, and though they chasten him, will not hearken unto them; then shall his father and his mother lay hold on him, and bring him out unto the elders of his city, and unto the gate of his place; and they shall say unto the elders of the city: This our son is stubborn and rebellious, he does not hearken to our voice; he is a glutton and a drunkard. And all the men of the city shall stone him with stones, that he die; so shall you put away the evil from your midst and all Israel shall hear, and fear. (Deuteronomy 21:18–21)

This is a very clear disciplinary policy: if a child does not respond to his parents' instructions and limits, the child is executed. The Sages, troubled by the severity of this sentence, made it almost impossible to declare a child so rebellious as to merit this punishment. Nonetheless, this passage testifies to the fact that there may come a time when parents throw up their hands in despair and turn their children over to the authorities, and the Torah apparently condones this course of action when a situation with a rebellious child becomes desperate enough.

How does a parent teach a child to "conquer the evil impulse," as *M. Pirkei Avot* (4:1) puts it? Our tradition teaches us that we should admonish our children strongly while they are growing up about what is appropriate behavior:

> "He that spares the rod, hates his son, but he that loves him chastens him betimes" (Proverbs 13:24). . . . The verse is to teach you that when a person refrains from chastising his son, the son will fall into evil ways, so that in the end the father will come to hate him. Thus it hap-

pened with Ishmael, whom his father loved so much that
he did not chastise him; then, when Ishmael fell into evil
ways, Abraham came to hate him so much that he cast
him out empty-handed from his house. What had Ishmael
done? When he was fifteen, he began to bring idols from
the marketplace, make merry with them, and worship
them the way he saw other people worship. [Upon seeing Ishmael playing so with the idols] "When Sarah saw
the son of Hagar the Egyptian playing" (and there is no
"playing" that is not idol worship) . . . she immediately
said to Abraham, "Cast out this bondwoman and her son"
(Genesis 21:10) lest my son learn his ways. Immediately,
"The thing was quite bad in Abraham's sight on account
of his son" (Genesis 21:11)—since he followed evil ways.
"And God said to Abraham, 'Let the thing not be bad in
your eyes concerning the boy . . . all that Sarah tells you
to do, you should listen to her" (Genesis 21:12). From
this you learn that Abraham was subordinate to Sarah in
prophecy. Immediately, "Abraham rose up early in the
morning, and took only bread and a bottle of water" (Genesis 21:14). This [the meager provisions with which
Ishmael was sent out] teaches you that Abraham hated
Ishmael for following evil ways and [therefore] sent him
and his mother Hagar out empty-handed when he cast
him out of his house. . . . And what was [Ishmael's] end?
After Abraham had driven him out, Ishmael sat at a cross-
roads and robbed people. (*Exodus Rabbah* 1:1)

This midrash seeks to explain why Abraham cast out his
son Ishmael. Of course, when we read the story in the
Torah, we find that Abraham is unwilling to send Ishmael
away. This exposition in the midrash paints Ishmael in a
more negative light, making Abraham's action in casting
the boy out more justifiable. It is worth noting that Abraham was extremely wealthy and therefore sending his son

out with only bread and water might well be seen as a sign of Abraham's disapproval. In any case, it provides an accurate picture of a lack of discipline and its effect: we end up hating the child we sought to pamper by not chastising her. In this case, Ishmael ends up rebelling against the very things Abraham holds dearest: monotheism (i.e., the rejection of paganism) and ethical behavior. The lesson appears to be that, had Abraham chastised Ishmael more strongly when he was young, Ishmael would not have become so loathsome to him later in life. Note that these passages do not indicate how to chastise one's child.

> We know how grueling it can be to be "the policeman" and constantly remind children to behave, say "please," do mitzvot, cooperate, and so forth. However, neglecting this parental duty will lead to unhappy children and parents who can't stand being around them. It's the old "pay now or pay later" dilemma. [JZA, SAA]

Limitations on Punishments: The Sages' View

We know that Jewish tradition advocates setting limits for our children. But how should we convey those limits? How do we discipline our children? The tradition is clear about how *not* to teach a child limits: we should not threaten the child with excessive punishment.

> It once happened that the son of Gordos of Lod fled from the school house and his father pointed to his ear [indicating that he would hit him on it] and he became fright-

ened of his father and destroyed himself in a pit. They went and asked Rabbi Tarfon and he said, "We do not withhold any [burial rites] from him."

It once happened that a young child of B'nei Brak broke a bottle on *Shabbat* and his father pointed to his ear [threatening to hit him on it] and the child became frightened of his father and destroyed himself in a pit. And they asked Rabbi Akiba [if the boy could have full burial rites] and he said, "We deny him nothing."

From this [these two cases] the Sages said, "A person should not threaten a child with boxing of the ears, but should hit him at once or be silent and say nothing." (*Semachot* 2:4–5)

The Sages are obviously aware of the harmful effects of verbal intimidation. A parent's approval and love are paramount in a child's mind: the child wants to please the parent and fears the parent's anger and displeasure. In fright, a child may run away rather than face a parent's anger and thereby come face-to-face with great danger.

Limitations on Punishment: Some Current Thoughts

Should a parent "hit him at once"? Does hitting accomplish anything constructive? In the context of the passage, a single hit was seen as mild punishment. We are concerned, however, that neither the passage from Proverbs (13:24, sparing the rod and hating the child) nor these passages from rabbinic literature be taken to imply that corporal punishment is the way to deal with rebellious children.

Support for corporal punishment remains strong in many sectors of this country and within the Jewish community. One Jewish parenting manual describes what the author believes are appropriate approaches to child raising, and states that if parents are "acting, when they hit their child, only out of concern for his welfare, hitting need not be either harmful or cruel." The author proceeds to give as an example a mother who "successfully" teaches her 4-year old not to say "*meshuga'at* (crazy)" by "hitting her gently on her hand." The passage continues to explain that the child "ran out of the room crying" and "cried for a long time," but didn't use the offending word again.[3]

To us, this example suggests why corporal punishment is potentially so harmful. The mother may feel better because she spoke quietly and hit gently, but the child didn't appreciate the subtlety. In addition, the next time the mother hits the child, she may not do so as gently. We wonder who taught the child the word meshuga'at *and whether others in the family reward her by laughing when she says it. Finally, we note that experimenting with "forbidden" words is characteristic of small children and, in a young child, is best dealt with by verbally indicating that this is undesirable behavior. [SAA, JZA]*

Corporal Punishment: A View from the Pediatric Community

Fortunately, the pediatric community is becoming aware of the negative effects of corporal punishment. The following commentary by Dr. Morris Wessel from the widely read medical journal *Pediatrics* does a better job than we could of answering supporters of corporal punishment.

Spanking or inflicting other forms of corporal punishment in response to exasperating behavior confuses a child who cannot comprehend why adults are treating him in this manner. All he knows is that adults whom he loves and trusts are attacking him, sometimes in an angry and violent manner. The immediate effect on the child ranges from mild embarrassment and feelings of worthlessness to permanent physical and psychological harm. There is also evidence which indicates that although corporal punishment may momentarily alter behavior, it is ineffective as a permanent solution to a child's difficulty in establishing the appropriate self-control necessary to please the adults who care for him.

Physical punishment, particularly when applied in anger, impairs a child's trust and confidence in the individuals he looks to for love, help, and guidance. It is humiliating and demeaning. It portrays the idea that might makes right and that size, brawn, and position in the adult world entitle one to inflict pain on younger and smaller individuals. The child suppresses his smoldering anger and resentment thinking "just wait until I get bigger. I'll beat up younger people just like you do." This idea becomes deeply embedded in the child's future character.

A physician, educator, or other professional child care worker who inflicts or sanctions corporal punishment, even with parental permission, misjudges his or her professional role and responsibility. . . . Pediatricians should be leading the movement to substitute nonviolent methods for corporal punishment. . . . No matter by whom administered, corporal punishment signifies a loss of control of the adult's feelings. When, as pediatricians, we allow corporal punishment, we condone child abuse.[4]

We agree with this statement wholeheartedly. Would one strike God's image? Then one should not strike a child or any other human being, for that matter. However, even the best parents may lose control. How can parents recover once they have hit a child? Learning to avoid situations that try the patience and learning to deal with their own guilt after hitting their children are important skills for parents to learn. If parents can learn techniques for self-control, they may be able to serve as role models for their children in this regard.

No one imagines that just sending a child to her room for "time out" is the answer to all discipline problems in children. Misbehavior has many causes and many potential responses. It's just that spanking is not one of the best responses, or even an effective response. When significant behavior problems occur, it's time to consider professional counseling.

How can you deal with your child when you feel so frustrated you consider hitting her? First of all, try and disengage until you, and she, have cooled off. Then, when you reengage, listen to what your child is saying and try to reflect what she is saying to you. Then, try to express, in a nonaccusing way, what you are feeling (of course, this requires that you be in touch with your own feelings). Ask your child to reflect back to you what you've said so that you know she understands. As each person feels listened to, often as not, the emotional heat is drained from the situation and the issue at hand can be dealt with more effectively. [JZA, SAA]

Social and Religious Skills

Almost every parent has experienced a child's perfect mimicking of some of her mannerisms. Our children watch us intently and use our behavior as a basis for their own. Therefore, it should not be surprising that the most effective way to teach our children is through the example we set. Whether we acknowledge it or not, our actions set the standard for our children in terms of ethical behavior, kindness, marital harmony, and so forth. The Sages were well aware that we are role models for our children. So, for example, they urge parents to be honest with their children lest they teach their children that lying is acceptable.

> Rabbi Zera said: A man should not say to a child, "I will give you something," and then not give it to him, because he will thus teach the child to lie, as it is said, "They teach their tongue to speak lies (Jeremiah 9:4)." (B. Sukkah 46b)

The verse from Jeremiah, in its context, appears to refer to people teaching their own tongues to lie. However, when taken by itself, this phrase could mean that people teach someone else's tongue to lie. And clearly, the Sages felt that lying to a child, even if the lie is nothing more than promising to give a child something and then failing to deliver, will teach a child to lie. If we want children to talk with us honestly and to know how to trust others, we must fulfill our promises to them.

Some actions cannot be mandated by legislation. In such cases, the Sages characterize the desired (or reviled) behavior as a course of action that will eventually be rewarded (or punished) by God.

Three the Holy One, blessed be He, loves: he who does
not become angry, he who does not become intoxicated,
and he who does not insist on his [full] rights. Three things
the Holy One, blessed be He, hates: he who speaks one
thing with his mouth and another thing in his heart; and
he who possesses evidence concerning his neighbor and
does not testify for him; and he who sees something
indecent in his neighbor and testifies against him alone.
(B. Pesachim 113b)

What does a good role model do? A good role model
controls her temper, controls her appetites, and controls
her pride. What does a poor role model do? A poor role
model speaks dishonestly, refuses to come to the aid of
a person who deserves it, and accuses someone simply
to make them look bad. (In a Jewish court, a minimum
of two qualified witnesses must come forward to testify
against a person. If only one person comes forward, that
testimony is inadmissible and therefore only serves to
defame the accused.) If we want to be loved by God, and
train our children to be loved by God, then we should be
self-controlled, honest, willing to help others, and not vin-
dictive. Not surprisingly, these attributes will also make
us beloved by our families and communities and ultimately raise our own self-esteem.

The laws in Judaism regarding lashon rara *("speaking
badly") are comprehensive. Speaking about other
people, in general, is a quick way to get yourself in
trouble and make enemies. Even if what you say
about someone else is true, Judaism frowns on your
saying it. And listening to gossip about others is considered to be a worse sin than spreading it. Why?
Because if no one would listen, no one would talk.*

When you listen to gossip you lend it credibility. [SAA, JZA]

Rabbi Akiba gave his own son the following, very practical, pieces of advice for getting along in the world:

> Our Rabbis taught: Seven things did Rabbi Akiba charge his son Rabbi Joshua: My son, do not sit and study at the highest point in town; do not dwell in a town whose leaders are scholars; do not enter your own house suddenly, and all the more your neighbor's house; and do not withhold shoes from your feet. Arise early and eat, in summer on account of the sun and in winter on account of the cold; treat your Sabbath like a weekday rather than be dependent on man, and strive to be on good terms with the man upon whom the hour smiles. (*B. Pesachim* 112a)

Rabbi Akiba urged his son not to study at the highest point in town lest people, frequently passing by, interrupt his study. He shouldn't live in a town run by scholars, since they are intent on studying and neglect the needs of the town. He should give warning when entering a house simply to be polite and to prevent those within from becoming startled. He should take care of his health by wearing shoes (protection from scorpions), rising early and eating breakfast. He shouldn't borrow money so that he could live a lavish lifestyle, even when it came to religious requirements. (One's Sabbath meal was to be more luxurious than one's weekday meals. Nonetheless, Rabbi Akiba taught that it is better to have a "weekday" style meal on *Shabbat* than to borrow money in order to have a fancier *Shabbat* dinner.) Finally, Rabbi Akiba urged his son to be on good terms with the rich persons in his town. In other words, he taught his son to look out for himself, study hard, be aware of his surroundings, take care of his health, be polite, be frugal, but not spurn good fortune.

We might find it odd that Rabbi Akiba, one of our most learned and pious Sages, would choose to give his son such practical wisdom as his core advice to him. And yet he reflected an important truth: as Jewish parents we are, of course, supposed to teach our children the religious wisdom of our tradition. Yet we should also teach them how to negotiate their way in the world at large.

> *Being a parent can be like being a coach. We care for our child as a whole person even as we work on specific skills with her. Rabbi Akiba is a good role model for this: his advice is balanced. He cares about his son as a whole person, not just about his Jewishness or his intellect.* [JZA, SAA]

Financial Obligations to Our Children

Occasionally parenting may seem to be primarily a check-writing activity. Camp tuition; skating, judo, music, and drawing lessons; clothes, toys, and games are all only part of the requirements of a well-rounded childhood. What are parents financially obligated to provide for their children? The list may seem endless to modern-day parents. For the Sages, it was considerably shorter. Parents are obligated to see that their children experience those *mitzvot* they are too young to observe themselves. We are also obligated to give them a Jewish education and teach them a way to earn money and help them to find a mate.

> What are a father's obligation regarding a son? [He is obligated] to circumcise him, to redeem him, and to teach him Torah, and to teach him a trade, and to marry him off to a woman. And there are those who say, [he is also obligated] to teach him to swim in the river. Rabbi Judah says, "Whoever does not teach his son a trade teaches him to be a robber." (*T. Kiddushin* 1:11)

The Sages work out their paradigm of parent–child relationships in terms of the father–son relationship. What must a father do for his son? He must see that he is ritually circumcised and, if the child is the firstborn, redeemed in a ceremony called *pidyon haben*, the redemption of the firstborn son. This custom is still practiced today by lay Israelites. (If either the father or mother is a member of a priestly family, i.e., Kohanim or Leviim, the parents do not have to redeem their firstborn sons, nor do they need to redeem their sons if they were born by cesarean section or if there was a previous miscarriage or abortion.) On the thirty-first day after the boy's birth, the father gives five silver coins to any Kohen. The Kohen may keep the coins, return them to the father if he is in need, or donate them to charity. A father is obligated to teach his son the Torah, and the obligations required in it. The father must also teach his son a trade, for if he does not, it is likened to teaching him to be a thief, because he'll have to make money somehow. Therefore, the father is obligated to teach his son to make a living honestly. Finally, he must see to it that his son marries. A further opinion is stated that he must also teach him to swim. Why? Because his life may depend on it.

In essence, then, what is it that parents are obligated to provide for their children? They must see that their children observe the *mitzvot* in their youth, and that they are prepared to live a productive, righteous life. When children are given their names, we wish for them a life of Torah (Jewish learning), *huppah* (marriage and family life), and *ma'asim tovim* (good deeds). It is the basis for living such a life that we are obligated to provide for our children.

Providing these opportunities for our children, and providing them with all the luxuries they desire, and which we wish to give them, may involve some sacrifice on our part.

> A person should always eat and drink less than his means allow, clothe himself in accordance with his means, and honor his wife and children more than his means allow, for they are dependent upon him and he is dependent upon Him who spoke and the world came into being. (*B. Hullin* 84b)

The Sages were aware that providing for one's family may involve some sacrifice. Now, since it is often the case that both mother and father work, we would imagine they are both obligated to indulge their children more than they indulge themselves. However, this passage must be placed in its context. The Sages wrote in an age when indulging one's children often meant feeding them better food than one fed oneself. The Sages surely did not mean that a child should be given every toy or piece of candy she desires. Every human being's desires are infinite and each of our bodies and resources are finite. We do our children a service when we make them aware, kindly but firmly, of this inherent tension in the human condition.

How do you say no to your children? It is not terribly easy. First, we can offer alternatives. "You can't have

*the 6-foot, $500 Barney doll, but you can have this
Barney game for $15." "You can have these $100 shoes
if you use some of your own money to pay for them
or you can have these $50 shoes for which we will pay
completely." We can also remind children of the consequences of their choices. "If you eat that candy, you
may have an upset stomach. How about a piece of fruit
or some yogurt instead?" We can also reward forbear-
ance or hard work. For example, if a child forgoes one
treat, we can take her on a special outing that she has
wanted.* [SAA, JZA]

The Sages were well aware that children can spend
money foolishly if they are overindulged and are not
taught the value of earning a living:

> R. Yohanon said: If one is left a fortune by his parents,
> and wishes to lose it, let him wear linen garments, use
> glassware, and engage workers and not be with them.
> (*B. Hullin* 84b)

Of course, the main thrust of this passage is that one
should not waste money on fancy clothes and knick-
knacks, nor should one place oneself in a position wherein
people will be tempted to give less work than they ought
to. In addition, the implication is that children who are
overindulged do not know the value of money and the
work it takes to earn it. The Sages seem to be saying,
"Treat your family well, but with moderation."

Protecting Our Children

From the material that we have studied to this point, it is
clear that parents are to protect their children. Accord-

ingly, in commenting on the obligation to teach a child
to swim, the Gemara makes it clear that we are to provide our children with the means to save their own lives:

> And some say, [He must teach him] to swim in water too.
> What is the reason?—His life may depend on it. (*B. Kid-
> dushin* 30b)

Just as we are obligated to care for our children, we are
obligated to ensure that they are able to protect themselves and their lives. If, as the passage suggests, we must
do what we can to teach our children things their lives
depend on, then we must teach them many things, including self-protection, avoidance of substance abuse (including tobacco), and appropriate sexual behavior.

> *Again, the question is how do we talk to our children
> about these topics? First, we need to learn the correct
> information on these issues. Pediatricians, Planned
> Parenthood and the local mental health association
> are good sources of information. (And we must take
> care to update ourselves periodically, since the infor-
> mation on these topics can change quickly.) Second,
> we need to be approachable. Children know when
> their parents are uncomfortable with their questions
> and you'd like your children to be able to ask you
> anything. Third, start at a young age. Letting children
> know that their bodies are private space that is to be
> respected and controlled by themselves is a lesson
> they can begin learning even in kindergarten.* [JZA,
> SAA]

An obligation parents have, sadly, is to teach their children how to protect themselves against physical and

sexual assault. This problem was not unknown to the Sages.

> Our Rabbis taught: . . . those that play with children delay the advent of the Messiah. . . . What is meant by "those that play with children"? If it be suggested: Those that practice pederasty [it could well be objected]: Are not such people subject to stoning [which is more severe than just delaying the Messiah]? If it be suggested: Those that practice onanism through external contact [it could be objected]: Are not such deserving destruction by flood?—The meaning rather is: Those that marry minors who are not capable of bearing children. (B. Niddah 13b)

This is a remarkable passage with contemporary relevance. This passage indicates that the Sages were aware of adults having anal intercourse with boys (pederasty) and masturbating on the bodies of children (onanism through external contact). This passage provides us with another example of the Sages wanting to condemn a course of action with their moral, as well as their legal, authority. Those who sexually abuse children in any way are deemed to delay the coming of the Messiah. The only discussion here is what form of sexual abuse is "legal" but nonetheless morally reprehensible. Pederasty and molestation are both illegal and are subject to two different sorts of death penalties, stoning and death by drowning that are carried out through a heavenly court, while marrying an extremely young girl and having intercourse with her was not illegal. Nonetheless, it was considered immoral and was strongly discouraged.

Sexual abuse of children is a national tragedy and a nightmare that haunts the lives of millions of Americans (mostly, but not entirely, women). It is not an aberration of television talk shows, but an ongoing disaster that has existed for thousands of years. Truly, those who sexually molest children delay the coming of an age when the world is at peace. The scars of childhood sexual abuse last a lifetime and the shock waves of these crimes are felt for generations.

What can be done? Each one of us can help by being aware of what is happening around us. Many children who are abused will try to tell an adult (teacher, classmate's parent, neighbor, rabbi, doctor) about the abuse. We must listen to these children. And we must teach our children about the privacy of their bodies. It may be difficult for us, as Jews, to face up to the fact that sexual abuse of children takes place in our community. Certainly, the Sages denied that it was a possibility:

> Israel is suspected of neither pederasty nor bestiality. (*B. Kiddushin* 82a)

Perhaps this reflects what the Sages *wished* were the case rather than what was reality. Certainly, and sadly, it is no longer true that Jews are not suspected of sexual abuse. Jews do sexually abuse children and batter their spouses.

> *We do not do our children any service when we deny that such things can and do happen. We, and our children, must be aware that such things do happen in the Jewish community and that when they do, we must come forward, report such incidents to the authorities, and work to make sure that they do not happen again. Working to help others heal is an important step in helping our community heal itself, too.* [SAA, JZA]

How Children Change
Their Parents' Relationship

Having children changes one's perception of oneself and of one's marriage partner. The stretch marks, the scars, the way gravity gradually makes its force manifest in the contours of one's body, leave indelible physical and psychological marks on a person, and the Sages were aware of this:

> When is a woman old? When she is called mother and doesn't mind. (*B. Niddah* 9a–b)

Hopefully, the benefits of motherhood outweigh its disadvantages. Nonetheless, understanding one's feelings about oneself and knowing that one's figure will never quite be what it was are part of giving up one's identity as a "girl" and taking on the roles of "adult" and "mother."

> *The cultural shift that occurs in the lives of parents is more gradual, but no less dramatic. Couples who had traveled, eaten out in fancy restaurants weekly, seen every recently released movie, and slept in on weekends soon find themselves traveling only to amusement parks, eating a great deal of pizza, seeing movies only on videocassette or on television, and arising at the crack of dawn (or earlier). When you know all the dialogue in* Mary Poppins *and know every permutation of "The Wheels on the Bus Go Round and Round," you realize how drastically things have changed. On the other hand, I have never heard anyone on her deathbed say, "I wish I'd seen more movies" or "I wish I'd spent more time at work." Yet you*

often hear "How quickly childhood disappears—I wish I'd enjoyed my children more when they were young." [JZA]

Many a parent, remarking on this cultural shift, exclaims, "Having children makes you stupid" (it doesn't). However, the Sages seemed to be aware of this apparent phenomenon:

> Rabbi Dosa ben Harkinas said: Late morning sleep, midday wine, children's chatter, and sitting in the assemblies of the ignorant remove a person from the world. (*M. Pirkei Avot* 3:14)

Rabbi Dosa ben Harkinas likens listening to children to indolence, drunkenness, and spending time with fools. In other words, spending time with one's children does prevent one from getting one's work accomplished. Working parents are constantly faced with this dilemma: wanting to relate to their child and also wanting to accomplish their work, be it work in an office or housework. Here we are presented with a rather one-sided view: spending time with children does take time away from work. On the other hand, spending time with one's children can be very rewarding and as important as working.

Having children can have positive, as well as negative, influences on a marital relationship. For example, children may try to help their parents get along more amicably:

> Rav was constantly tormented by his wife. If he told her, "Prepare me lentils," she would prepare for him small peas; [and if he asked for] small peas, she prepared him lentils. When his son Hiyya grew up he gave her [his father's instructions] in the reverse order. Rav said to him

[Hiyya], "Your mother has improved!" He [Hiyya] said to him [Rav], "It was I who reversed [your orders] to her." He [Rav] said to him, "This is what people say: 'Your own offspring teaches you reason'; you, however, must not continue to do so; for it is said, 'They have taught their tongue to speak lies, they weary themselves to commit iniquity' (Jeremiah 9:4)." (*B. Yebamot* 63a)

Children are keenly aware of their parents' relationship to each other. Clearly Hiyya knew that his mother was tormenting his father and purposefully serving him exactly what he didn't want for dinner. So Hiyya stepped in and, when Rav said he wanted lentils, Hiyya would tell his mother, "Dad wants small peas." Poor Rav! He thought his wife was becoming kinder, but Hiyya disabuses him of that delusion. And once he finds out what is going on, he forbids his son to continue his diplomacy for fear that he would learn to lie habitually. However, it is noteworthy that it apparently takes Rav a long time to figure out what was going on. This passage shows that children frequently try to serve as peacemakers between their parents. In general, this is not a good role for children, but it is a common one. Once Rav finds out about it, he correctly puts a stop to it. Rav seems to understand that his son may feel responsible for the tension between Rav and his wife and may have been trying to let his son know that he is not the cause of the discord.

Stepparents and Stepchildren

"Blended families," as stepfamilies are often called today, can experience some tensions that are different from those felt by other families. The Sages seem to be aware that such tensions would exist and that it was possible that parents would favor their biological children over their stepchildren. For example, the Sages take it for granted that a stepfather would not want to provide as much monetary support for a stepchild as for his own child.

[The reason a pregnant woman may not marry someone other than the fetus's father] is because she might conceive again, her milk would become turbid and she might thereby cause the death of the child. If so this applies in the case [of the man's own child also]! His own child she would sustain with eggs and with milk. Would she not sustain her own child [from the first father, if she remarried] also with eggs and with milk? Her [second] husband would not give her the means. [He would say] Let her claim it from the heirs (i.e., from the first husband's family). (*B. Yebamot* 42a–b)

We think of issues involving stepfamilies as recent ones. However, as this passage suggests, these problems existed in ancient days, as well. In this passage, the Rabbis are concerned with what would happen if a pregnancy forced a woman to stop nursing. After recognizing that this could happen regardless of who the woman was married to, either her original husband or a second husband, the Sages indicate that their real worry is that a stepfather would refuse to pay for food for his stepchild, whereas they assume a natural father would pay for such sustenance.

What are a stepparent's obligations toward her stepchildren? Obviously, this question must be answered on a case-by-case basis, taking into account factors such as how much time the children spend in the household, how old the children are, and what their feelings are about their parent's remarriage. Of course, the more a child is loved and nurtured, no matter by whom, the better off that child will be. While a step-parent cannot, and should not, attempt to replace a child's natural parent, she can provide additional mature insight and guidance for a child. [JZA, SAA]

Concluding Thoughts on Parent–Child Relationships

The Sages' concept of the parent–child relationship seems to be based on the idea of stewardship. Our children must be shepherded and shaped; they are to be provided with the means to function as independent human beings. But until they can function on their own, parents are to guide them and guard them. It is to the time of independence and separation to which we next turn our attention: the turbulent time of adolescence.

III

Separation

9

Adolescence and Jewish Parenting

From Jewish mysticism we learn of the idea of *tsim-tsum*. In essence, this is the concept that God contracts God's presence in order to give us more responsibility as we mature spiritually and morally. In many ways, this is a wonderful model for parents of adolescents: they should "contract" as their children become more and more capable. Nonetheless, parents do not disappear during adolescence and their input is extremely important in communicating appropriate values in terms of a child's general health and, in particular, in teaching their child about assimilation, dating, sex, and drugs.

General Nutrition and Health

Though adolescent children may not wish to be guided by their parents concerning their diet, they still must be helped to eat healthfully. The Sages had some things to say about children's nutrition that are valid today. For example, the Sages urged their daughters to drink their milk.

> He who wishes his daughter to have a bright complexion, let him, on the approach of her maturity, feed her with young fowls and give her milk to drink. (B. Ketubot 59b)

The advice given in this passage is sound. Recent studies have shown that the peak period when children acquire calcium to strengthen their bones is during early adolescence, as they are going through puberty. By late adolescence, a girl will have acquired over 90 percent of the total bone calcium she will ever have. Therefore it's a good idea to encourage an adequate intake of high calcium-containing foods such as dairy products in girls "approaching maturity" (although it won't cause a "bright complexion"). For children who don't like or can't tolerate dairy products, it is important to discuss with one's pediatrician or a nutritionist possible alternative sources of calcium and other minerals (such as some vegetables and calcium-fortified juices). Concern about osteoporosis, however, undoubtedly was not behind the Sages' advice. Osteoporosis is not described in rabbinic literature, although there are references to lameness in the elderly that may be related to osteoporosis (e.g., Leviticus Rabbah 18:1).

It is not only modern parents who try to make their children take better care of themselves. Rav also urged his son to take care of his health.

> Rav said to his son Hiyya. Do not take drugs, don't leap over a sewer, don't have your teeth pulled, don't provoke serpents. (B. Pesachim 113a)

The traditional explanation of this passage has to do with the "commonsense medicine" of the Sages' day. The first statement, do not take drugs, is one we would concur with: Rav is concerned that his son will fall into the habit of taking drugs, so it is best not to start with them at all. However, we should note that there is a difference between taking drugs and abusing them. The ocasional use of pain medication when appropriate does not lead to addiction, and parents should not deny their children the benefits of such medication. The admonition against leaping over a sewer and having your teeth pulled has to do with the Sages' belief that these practices were bad for one's eyesight. Finally, the admonition not to provoke a serpent can be taken as a metaphor: don't tempt trouble. It can also be seen as a wise piece of interpersonal advice. Some persons are like serpents and it is best not to tangle with them.

Assimilation and Peer Pressure

One of the most pressing problems facing Jewish parents today is how to encourage their children to date Jews in order to prevent intermarriage. Parental disapproval is one of the most powerful preventatives to interdating and intermarrying when coupled with a logical rationale as to why the continuity of the Jewish people is important. If parents convey, through direct communication and through example (i.e., practicing Judaism) that Judaism is central to their lives and make it central to the lives of their children, they make it more likely that their children will marry Jews. It is as if there were a "dose response" in the control of intermarriage. The more Judaism is practiced in the home, the more Jewish education a child is given, the more a child goes to Jewish camps and/or Israel or participates in Jewish youth groups, the more likely it is that the child will marry a Jew.[1]

As parents, we must be able to articulate for our children why Judaism is not only different from other religions but better than other religions for Jews. We are certainly not advocating denigrating someone else's faith for them. It can be explained with the following analogy. Our spouses are the ideal ones for us, but they probably would not be the ideal mates for someone else. Just so is Judaism ideal for us, but that does not mean that other religions are not good for other people. But we must be clear that Judaism is better for us. It is the faith that fits our spirits, our intellects, and our lives. The belief in one God, and one God only, is challenging, but satisfies the intellect. Judaism is a religion that gives us personal responsibility for our lives. [SAA, JZA]

When making college choices, families can consult *The Hillel Guide to Jewish Life on Campus*, published yearly by the B'nai Brith Organization. Using this resource, which gives information on the number of Jewish students, the availability of kosher food, and the amount of Jewish programming on many college campuses, parents and children can work together to choose a college that is suitable. In addition, teaching our children to keep kosher, including when they go away to college, not only encourages the observance of an important *mitzvah*, but serves as a way to constantly remind our children of their Jewish identity. Certainly the Sages saw keeping kosher as a way to minimize intermarriage.

> One time Rabbi [Yehudah HaNasi] went out into the field,
> and a heathen brought before him a loaf baked in a large
> oven from a *se'ah* (about 2 gallons) of flour. Rabbi said:
> How beautiful is this loaf; why should the Sages have
> thought fit to prohibit it! "Why should the Sages have
> thought fit to prohibit it?" As a safeguard against [inter]-
> marriages! (*B. Avodah Zarah* 35b)

The large, beautiful, prohibited loaf of bread was baked by an idolator (i.e., a follower of one of the ancient gods such as Zeus or Hermes) and is therefore forbidden to Jews. It is clear why this bread is prohibited. The Sages knew if you couldn't eat their bread you would be less likely to meet idolators and much less likely to want to live with one. There are numerous prohibitions in the Talmud regarding avoiding contact with idolators. We currently do not view followers of modern religions such as Christianity or Islam as "idolators." Nonetheless, it is important to note that the Sages' purpose was to encourage Jews to maintain a separate identity even while living in a society in which other beliefs predominated.

We need only think about social life in a modern university setting to see how important keeping kosher would be in reducing one's likelihood to intermarry. Much of one's social life at college revolves around where one is assigned to eat. If your child keeps kosher and eats in the kosher dining hall, then morning, noon, and night he will be with Jews who have chosen to keep kosher. The chances that your child will end up dating another Jew are therefore much higher. Students who cook for themselves have the opportunity to invite fellow Jewish students over for dinner and vice versa.

Of course, a child may keep kosher yet still succumb

to peer pressure to do foolish things, particularly drink alcohol or use drugs. It used to be thought that Jews did not have problems with drinking or drugs. Unfortunately, this is surely not the case today. Just as one must explicitly convey to one's child that intermarrying is not appropriate, one must explicitly teach one's child not to abuse drugs and alcohol. And just as religious values are best taught by setting a good example, so children are likely to follow our own practices regarding drugs and alcohol.

> *The implicit message that many parents give, that it is acceptable for one's child to have sex with multiple partners while young or that it is permissible for teenagers to drink alcohol, ignores the dangers associated with these behaviors. Similarly, old adages that imply that dating and sex with non-Jewish partners are acceptable, because in the end the child will marry a Jew, should be discarded as the errant nonsense they so patently are.* [JZA, SAA]

Rabbinic Insights into Alcoholism and Substance Abuse

In talking with our children, we might use Rabbi Judah as an example of how alcohol is used properly by Jews.

> A certain matron said to Rabbi Judah, "A teacher and a drunkard!" [his face was always bright red]. He said to her, "You may well believe me that I taste [no wine] but that of Kiddush and Havdalah and the four cups of Passover, on account of which I have to bind my temples from Passover until Shavuot [i.e., for 7 weeks]." (*B. Nedarim* 49b)

Apparently, Rabbi Judah had an extremely red face, which caused the woman in the story to think he was a lush. The opposite is, in fact, the case. When does Rabbi Judah use alcohol? Only when it is ritually mandated on Friday evening (*Kiddush*), at the end of *Shabbat* (at *Havdalah*, the ceremony which ends the Sabbath), and on Passover when we are to have four cups of wine. It is interesting that he does not drink liquor on Purim, even though it was already customary to do so in the Sages' day. This may be one way to frame the entire topic of alcohol consumption for our adolescents: it is used to make moments holy. Alcohol is to be used in moderation, in settings where it has a meaning beyond "getting high." In particular, it should be emphasized that drinking and driving do not mix. After all, Rabbi Judah did not have to drive after drinking four glasses of wine at the seder.

It may well be impossible to keep our children from doing foolish things when they are teenagers, since they may not understand the long-term consequences of their actions, no matter how long and loud we lecture them.

> And Rabbi Isaac said: What means the verse, "For child-hood and youth are vanity" (Ecclesiastes 11:10)? The things a man does in his youth blacken his face in his old age. (*B. Shabbat* 152a)

Today, this passage could refer to inappropriate sexual behavior in youth coming back to haunt a person in later days. Sadly, teenagers often do not believe that disease or death will come to them as a result of sexual promiscuity or substance abuse. They feel they are invincible and invulnerable. Today, in an age of AIDS, the Sages' teaching about the long-term consequences of youthful foolishness is even more true than it may have been previously. Perhaps the best we can do is love our children, make them understand their worth to us and to God, and teach them to value themselves. Above all, we must talk to them about the risks that are attendant on their behavior. Parents who feel embarrassed talking to their children about sex can ensure that their children have access to an adult they *can* talk with, such as a pediatrician, rabbi, teacher, or counselor who is qualified to discuss these topics.

> *Perhaps the most important thing we can teach our children is that when their gut tells them something isn't right, to follow their instincts. One 16-year-old of our acquaintance was at a party when, early in the evening, the other kids there began to drink and become rowdy. His gut told him that things weren't going right and he left, which takes no small amount of courage. The next day, he discovered that the others at the party had later bashed in many car windows in a drunken spree and he was quite glad he missed this episode and the ensuing trouble they encountered. The moral of the story: teach your children to trust their instincts about right and wrong behavior and that it's better to go with one's inner voice than the voices of the crowd.* [SAA, JZA]

Tension and Independence between Parent and Child

Childhood can be seen as a series of ever more sophisticated steps that the child takes toward independence. And part of each step is a child's testing his parents. Of course, parents test their children, too. For example, Rav Huna wanted to know if his son Rabbah could practice the precept "Honor your parents" even when his father was destroying valuable property.

> Rav Huna tore up silk in the presence of his son Rabbah, saying, "I will go and see whether he flies into a temper or not." But perhaps he would get angry and then he [Rav Huna] would violate [the precept], "You shall not put a stumbling block before the blind" (Leviticus 19:14). (B. Kiddushin 32a)

The injunction against putting a stumbling block before the blind is interpreted by the Sages as a general prohibition against taking advantage of a person's blind spots. Therefore, the Sages condemn Rav Huna for testing his grown son's temper, which they see as tempting him to sin. That is, testing another person is something the Sages are against since it is, in a sense, tempting fate. This attitude can be applied to parents and children alike: testing limits may not be a productive exercise in human relations.

When is a child independent of his parents? Of course, children are always bound to honor their parents. However, parents are responsible for their children's behavior until they reach their majority. After this point, the child is independent of his parents: any sins he commits are his responsibility. At this point parents may sigh with relief, as did Isaac and Rebeccah:

> "And the boys [Jacob and Esau] grew" (Genesis 25:27). R. Levi said: They were like a myrtle and wild rose-bush growing side by side; when they grew to maturity, one yielded its fragrance and the other its thorns. So for thir-

teen years both went to school and came home from
school. After this age, one went to the house of study and
the other to idolatrous shrines. Rabbi Eleazar said: A person must care for his child until the age of thirteen; thereafter he must say, "Blessed is He who has now freed me
from this responsibility." (*Genesis Rabbah* 63:10)

The Sages are here commenting on the entirety of this
verse from Genesis:

And the boys grew; and Esau was a cunning hunter, a
man of the field; and Jacob was a quiet man, dwelling in
tents. (Genesis 25:27)

The Sages wonder why the boys are paired in the first
phrase of this sentence, "and the boys grew," and then
so sharply distinguished in the second part of the sentence. This midrash from *Genesis Rabbah* suggests that,
until they grew up, i.e., reached the age of 13, although
they had different personalities, they both behaved appropriately. Their father and mother, Isaac and Rebeccah,
were responsible for them and saw that they went to
school. However, after they reached their majority, when
they could no longer be coerced by their parents, they
each went their separate way: Esau to a life of hunting
(as in the biblical text) and idol worship (as in the midrash)
and Jacob to a life of contemplation and study. Rabbi
Eleazar then declares a general rule. Up until the age of
13 we must raise and guide children; at that time one says,
with relief, "Thank God I am no longer responsible for this
child!" Alternatively, at this point parents may sigh with
gratitude and pride, saying simply, "Thank God for this
child!"

When would one be able to genuinely say that prayer today? When the child graduates from high school? From college? From graduate school? Gets married? We may be legally responsible for our children only until they are 18 years old, but our true obligation lasts much longer. And even though we may no longer hold ourselves, or be held by others, legally responsible for a child's errant behavior, a parent's love and aid are probably always appreciated by a child, no matter how old they are. [JZA, SAA]

I sent my parents a copy of my first article published in a medical journal with a note of thanks (I figure that article cost them a small fortune in tuition, etc.). They framed it and have it—with the note of thanks—prominently displayed in their house. [SAA]

Dating and Love

How do you know when you're really in love? Can you love more than one person at the same time? When do you know you've met the person you should marry? These are some of the questions adolescents ask most frequently about relationships. The Sages, naturally, had answers to those questions. They prized the stable, committed, monogamous relationship associated with marriage. Such a relationship was, in miniature, a reflection of Israel's relationship with God: one people and one God. (This is one reason why idolatry, the worship of many gods, is so often likened to promiscuity in rabbinic literature.)

So how *do* you know when you're really in love? Two people are in love when they are not merely sexually attracted to each other, but when they are truly concerned about each other's welfare.

All love that depends on a [specific] thing, [when the] thing ceases, [the] love ceases; and [all love] that does not depend on a [specific] thing, never ceases. Which is the [kind of] love that depends on a [specific] thing? Such as was the love of Amnon for Tamar; and [which is the kind of love] that does not depend on a [specific] thing? Such was the love of David and Jonathan. (*M. Pirkei Avot* 5:19)

The "specific" thing mentioned here seems to refer to overwhelming sexual desire for another person, an attraction to their beauty, not to their inner self. That this attraction is not genuine love is shown by the example of the desire Amnon felt for his half-sister Tamar. He tricked her into visiting him in his private chambers and then raped her. Immediately thereafter, we read:

Then Amnon hated her with exceeding great hatred; for the hatred wherewith he hated her was greater than the love wherewith he had loved her. And Amnon said unto her: Arise, be gone. And she said to him: Not so, because this great wrong in putting me forth is worse than the other that you did unto me. But he would not hearken unto her. (2 Samuel 13:15–16)

This is an obvious example of a destructive emotion that is not true love. Amnon's desire for the beautiful Tamar obsessed him. However, once he had raped her, he hated himself and her and threw her out of his chambers. (Amnon is later killed by Tamar's brother, Absalom, in retribution for his crime.) Such passionate emotion, which destroys both parties, is not love.

So, then, what is true love? The phrase that describes the love of Jonathan, King Saul's son, for David is "a love of the soul" (1 Samuel 18:1 and 20:17). Such a love is the love of best friends for each other, rather than a love based on sexual attraction. When you value someone as much as you value yourself, when you help that person when they are in trouble, as Jonathan helped David, when you have the ability to spend time with that person and enjoy it—that is true love, according to the Sages. It seems that, in this passage from *Pirkei Avot*, the Sages may even be saying that being overly sexually attracted to someone can interfere with true love. True love, they seem to say, means you should be friends long before you are appropriately lovers with another person.

Can you love more than one person romantically at the same time? That, actually, is not the relevant question. The real question is what you do about such feelings if you have them. Expressing the importance of faithfulness to our children and being role models of faithfulness provide our children with important guidance. While our children may understand these lessons implicitly, they may like to have them expressed explicitly, as well. I will never forget a dinner we had with a friend of ours and his two adolescent boys. We began talking about the things that were most important to us and we asked him the sort of pointed questions children sometimes hesitate to ask their parents, such as "What do you pray about?" In the course of the conversation he said explicitly that being unfaithful to his wife was something he would simply never do or that was even in the realm of conceivable reality for him. You could see in his sons' eyes and their nodding heads that this information was directly internalized. It would probably have been hard for him to bring this up in direct conversation with his sons, but

being asked in their presence helped him give them
an important lesson. So perhaps your friends can help
you express yourself about these matters. [JZA, SAA]

Why Teenagers Date People
Who Drive Their Parents Crazy

Why is it that a teenager often brings home a long line of dates that seem totally inappropriate? Perhaps one reason is that these dates are different, exotic, and therefore exciting. Of course the ancillary benefit—that this drives their parents crazy—is probably also a plus. Ancient parents, like modern ones, had to deal with this phenomenon:

Rabbi Akiba was a shepherd of Ben Kalba Savua. His [Kalba Savua's] daughter, seeing how modest and noble [the shepherd] was, said to him, "Were I to be betrothed to you, would you go [away to study at] the academy?" He said to her, "Yes." She was secretly betrothed to him and she sent him away. When her father heard [what she had done] he drove her from his house and forbade her by a vow to have any benefit from his estate.

[Rabbi Akiba] went, and spent twelve years at the academy. When he returned home he brought with him twelve thousand disciples. [While in his home town] he heard an old man saying to her, "How long will you lead the life of living widowhood?" She said to him, "If he would listen to me he would spend [in study] another twelve years." Said [Rabbi Akiba], "It is then with her consent that I am acting," and he went again and spent another twelve years at the academy. When he returned he brought with him twenty-four thousand disciples. His wife heard [of his arrival] and went out to meet him. Her neighbors said to her, "Borrow some [respectable] clothes and put them on," but she replied: "A righteous man knows the life of his beast" (Proverbs 12:10). On approaching him she fell upon her face and kissed his feet. [Not knowing who she was,] his attendants were about to thrust her aside, when [Rabbi Akiba] cried to them, "Leave her alone, [for what is] mine and [what is] yours are hers."

Her father, on hearing that a great man had come to town said, "I shall go to him; perchance he will invalidate my vow [against my daughter]." When he came to him [Rabbi Akiba] said to him [Kalba Savua], "Would you have made your vow if you had known that he was a great man?" He said to him [Rabbi Akiba], "[Had he known] even one chapter or even one single *halakhah* [I would not have made the vow]." He [Rabbi Akiba] said to him, "I am the man." The other fell upon his face and kissed his feet and also gave him half of his wealth. (*B. Ketubot* 62b–63a)

Before we examine what this story has to say about adolescent mating behavior, let us analyze it for its plain meaning. First, we see it is arranged in a classic, tripartite way. People become more and more separated from each other as the story progresses. Rachel rebels against her wealthy and powerful father by becoming attracted to and marrying a poor, illiterate shepherd. Her father casts her out, impoverishing her. Then she sends her husband off to study at the academy and fulfill his potential. Thus she is left alone, without the company of her father or her husband. Yet she seems perfectly content and we wonder whether one thing—perhaps the *main* thing—that she got out of her relationship with Akiba was a means of separating from her father so that she could develop some independence. Certainly, as the story progresses she gives evidence of being satisfied living a life apart from her husband. And clearly, Rabbi Akiba is satisfied with the situation, as well. After Rabbi Akiba has fulfilled his potential as a great Sage and Rachel has established an identity independent of her father and her husband, the relationships in the story can be resumed in more healthy forms. Rabbi Akiba and Rachel are reunited, he giving her the credit for his success. Kalba Savua shows that he regrets the rash way he cast his daughter out and is able to make amends. Thus, the transition from dependent child to independent adult is facilitated by this marriage that appears grossly inappropriate at first blush.

While we know that Rabbi Akiba will turn out to be a great Sage and that Rachel is making a terrific match, we can still sympathize with poor Kalba Savua. Here he was, one of the three richest men in Jerusalem. Surely he had great plans for his daughter to marry someone like himself, i.e., rich and powerful. And who does she run off with? An illiterate, penniless shepherd. Clearly Rachel was not only choosing an illustrious husband for herself, even if only she could see his potential greatness, she was also rebelling against her father.

Is this an effective form of rebellion? Certainly, it is a popular form. However, perhaps parents can encourage their children to rebel, to gain their independence, by relying on their own inner strengths and talents, rather than relying on a relationship to help pry themselves loose. For if a relationship is based solely on separating from parents, once the rebellion and separation are accomplished, there may be nothing left to hold the relationship together. Perhaps it is better to rebel through personal achievement than through romantic relationship.

It is important to emphasize that although we do not support intermarriage (and do not perform them without conversion of the non-Jewish partner), we do not advocate abandoning a child who has intermarried. Try to help your children clarify for themselves what kind of house they will have and what their limits are. If they suggest that they will bring their children up in both religions or boys in one religion and girls in another, don't panic. Help them tease out how this will work later on in life. If they want to have a brit milah and a baptism for their boys, ask if they will have a confirmation and bar mitzvah ceremony, too, and the illogical nature of their decision may become clear to them. Help them elucidate what is important to them and let them know in the kindest way possible that they may think that they love this person so much that they are willing to give up everything, but that when children are involved, suddenly some things are not so easy to give up. Also, urge them to learn about each other's faiths and figure out what values they really want to exercise in their home. [JZA]

Marriage at an Early Age

The Sages prized marriage and urged their children to marry at as young an age as possible. In this way, they hoped to channel their children's sexual energies in appropriate ways.

It was taught in the school of Rabbi Ishmael: Until a person reaches the age of twenty, the Holy One sits and waits expectantly: "When will this man take a wife?" But when the young man reaches the age of twenty and has still not wed, He says, "May the bones of this one be blasted."

Rav Hisda said: Why am I superior to my colleagues [in learning]? Because I wed at sixteen. Had I wed at fourteen, I would have been able to say to Satan, "An arrow in your eye (i.e., I defy you!)!"

Rava said to Rabbi Nathan bar Ammi: While you have power over your son, when he is between sixteen and twenty-two (some say, between 18 and 24) get him married. (B. Kiddushin 29b–30a)

The Sages worried that a young man's *yetser hara*, his impulse to have sexual relations, would occupy his time and thoughts if it were not given a legitimate outlet through marriage. Therefore, they urged young men to marry early. We note once more that the *yetser hara* is not something to be denied. It is something to be controlled. Adolescents do have the urge to have sexual relationships. This urge can be controlled but it will not disappear through an act of will, nor would we wish it to do so. After all, we want the generations to march forward.

Today, with the inherent risks associated with sexual promiscuity, we need to emphasize abstinence for our adolescents. Recognizing that teens may have difficulty abstaining from sexual relations, it may not be appropriate to always encourage our children to delay marriage or the formation of a committed, monogamous relationship until their education is completed. We may want to allow, or even encourage, them to marry earlier rather than later, in line with the Sages' advice (albeit not at age 14). This commitment need not prohibit completion of a child's educational and career objectives. In addition, by encouraging abstention from sexual relations until marriage and by accepting the idea that marriage may take place at an earlier age, we may reestablish the link between being able to maintain a mature relationship and earning the privilege, as it were, of having sexual relations.

The Sages believed that in a long-term, committed, monogamous relationship, one could find great happiness.

> Any man who has no wife lives without joy, without blessing, and without goodness . . . without Torah . . . without peace. . . .
>
> Our Rabbis taught: Concerning a man who loves his wife as himself, who honors her more than himself, who guides his sons and daughters in the right path and arranges for them to be married near the onset of their puberty, Scripture says, "And you shall know that your tent is in peace" (Job 5:24). . . . Any man who has no wife is no proper man. (*B. Yebamot* 62b–63a)

This, then, may be the Sages' definition of love: a committed relationship that enables the partners to experience joy, blessing, goodness, Torah, and peace.

Birth Control and Abortion

The issues of birth control and abortion are ones that often need to be discussed with adolescents. Since our aim in this volume is not an exploration of Jewish law, but rather a presentation of sources from rabbinic literature, we will explore those sources. However, each individual case is different and Jewish law presents a wide range of possible solutions to difficult problems. Therefore, each family

should consult with its own rabbi or come to its own con-
clusions starting, perhaps, with a book such as David M.
Feldman's *Marital Relations, Birth Control and Abor-
tion in Jewish Law* (New York: Schocken, 1968) or
Abraham S. Abraham's *The Comprehensive Guide to
Medical Halachah* (New York: Feldheim, 1990).

As we already noted (*T. Niddah* 2:6), birth control is
permitted when pregnancy would harm the mother. Currently, there are relatively few situations in which a pregnancy might be deemed risky to the mother's life wherein
birth control, abortion, or preterm delivery would be necessary. These would principally involve women with serious chronic illnesses such as severe heart disease. A situation commonly faced today is that in which a mother has
developed life-threatening symptoms from a disease referred to as pregnancy-induced hypertension. In this
poorly understood disorder, pregnancy leads to high
maternal blood pressure and potential damage to the
maternal kidneys and other vital organs. In this situation, although treatment may often help the condition,
it is occasionally necessary to induce the delivery to
protect the mother, even if the baby will be extremely
premature.

*In this era, ensuring that one's sexually active adoles-
cent child is informed regarding appropriate contraception and "safe" sex is mandatory and failure to
do so is life threatening. A number of contraceptive options are available that are appropriate for adolescents, and these should be pursued with an appropriate medical caregiver. How much better for the
sexually active adolescent to be able to discuss these
issues with his parents than have to secretly go to a*

health center or drugstore and figure things out on his own. [SAA]

As with so many other complicated issues, the Sages present many points of view regarding abortion in rabbinic literature. These attitudes stem from one of Judaism's most basic values: a respect for, and treasuring of, life. However, the Sages also felt that the fetus was only potential life, while the mother did have an actual life that took precedence over the fetus's. So, for example, if a woman experienced a difficult birth, the fetus's life could be sacrificed for the mother's.

> The woman that suffers a hard birth process, the fetus may be cut into pieces while in her womb and they bring it out limb by limb because her life takes precedence over his. [But if] the majority [of his body] has emerged, we do not touch him for one life does not supersede another life. (*M. Oholot* 7:6)

One must remember that neither forceps nor safe cesarean sections were available when this teaching was formulated and that the Sages were describing a situation that does not occur today when many other options are available for dealing with a fetus that cannot be delivered routinely.

Recognizing that young women facing this decision may need some further practical guidance, we note that the Israeli Parliament passed a law in 1977 allowing abortions in the following circumstances: if a mother is under 16 or over 40; if the pregnancy resulted from incest, rape, or was out of wedlock; if it can be determined that the child would be born physically or emotionally handicapped; if the birth would injure the physical or emotional health of the mother.[2] As was mentioned above, rabbinic literature and Jewish law offer a wide range of opinions on this topic that must be considered in each individual case. No universal pronouncements will suffice: each woman must examine this issue for herself.

We support the right of every woman to have a safely performed abortion if she chooses this option. As debates rage over such issues as parental notification laws, we encourage parents of adolescents to ensure that their sons and daughters know that they can approach them if the need arises to discuss these matters regardless of "laws" on parental notification.

Abortion is probably never a beautiful choice. It always means something has gone wrong. Either contraception wasn't used, or it failed, or there is a problem with the pregnancy. However, it is often the well-thought-out choice for adolescents faced with an unplanned pregnancy. Having a baby can seriously affect an adolescent's plans for her life and her future. Adolescents who choose to terminate an unplanned pregnancy deserve their parents' support and love.

Other options need to be considered as well. I remember very clearly as a medical student seeing a patient, a college student, who chose to continue with an unplanned pregnancy and place the infant for adoption. For her, this was the best choice and she felt very strongly about it. The decisions adolescents face regarding unplanned pregnancies are difficult. Therefore, a parent who will listen instead of condemn or demand a certain course of action is probably needed more at such a time than at any other.

We speak, of course, as parents of preschoolers. We know that we can respond to our 2-year-old picking up a glass of juice and tossing it on the carpet without losing our cool. How we'll deal with adolescent problems remains to be seen. But it can't hurt to think about how we hope we'll respond. [SAA, JZA]

How to Communicate Values as a Jewish Parent

A parent faced, for example, with a pregnant teenage daughter or a son who had impregnated a girl might want to rant, rave, or cry. These reactions, however normal, may not be the most helpful in this, or any other, difficult situation. One paradigm for structuring a conversation about difficult dilemmas may come from the watchword of our faith: the Shema (Deuteronomy 6:4). Each word of the Shema can be taken as a step in a communication process with our children, as outlined here.

1. *Shema*: "Listen." This is the first important step in the communication process. We must listen to the content and the emotion of what our children are saying to us. We must allow them to speak and vent their own feelings and fears. If at all possible, before we do anything else, we should try to reflect back to them an accurate understanding of their situation and their emotions before we continue the conversation so that they feel heard, and therefore calmed.

2. *Yisrael*: "Israel." Once we have listened, then we can consider what Judaism says about the issue at hand.

We can take comfort and guidance from the wisdom of our traditions.

3. *Adonai*: "God." This name for God indicates God's merciful, empathetic aspect. Once we have listened and learned, then we should consider the situation with all the mercy and understanding we can show.

4. *Eloheinu*: "Our God." This name for God denotes God's more judgmental aspect. If our children have disappointed us, we are allowed to express this to them.

5. *Adonai*: "God." Once we have dealt with these feelings of judgment, disappointment, or disapproval we should return to mercy and empathy. In other words, for every judgmental word there should be two merciful ones.

6. *Ehad*: "One." All these steps have as their goal the honest expression of feeling in a way that is not hurtful to either party so that they can stay connected and in their relationship, that is, one.

Concluding Thoughts
on Adolescence and Jewish Parenting

It may be that as our children grow and become more independent that some pain is inevitably associated with relinquishing control over their lives. And yet, just as we could not stop them from falling in their quest to master standing and walking as toddlers, we cannot stop our older children from mastering the world for themselves and, in the process, unavoidably encountering a few hard knocks along the way. All we can do is provide them with a firm knowledge of who they are and how important they are to us, and know that the most rebellious teenagers often become the most conservative adults.

> *I was one of the worst-behaved children in my religious school. I tormented the teachers and was as rude as possible. I often contemplate God's justice: now I am a rabbi who must frequently deal with rude, misbehaving children in religious school. It gives me some measure of peace knowing, as I look on the worst-behaved child, that this may one day be a colleague of mine.* [JZA]

10

When a Child Dies

Throughout this book, we have mostly spoken of the normal course of childhood. We conclude by turning our attention to an important topic that, mercifully, does not touch as many of our lives as it did in ancient times. Yet to ignore the fact that children die would not serve parents, or our tradition, well. Indeed, rabbinic literature has many wise things to say on this topic. The insights of our tradition may be especially important since we are much less prepared to face the death of a child than parents probably were in ancient days.

We spend endless time in medical school learning how to care for our patients. Yet I can't remember receiving a single lecture, having a single discussion, or ever having an examination relating to how to deal with dying patients or with grieving families. To varying degrees, every physician must deal with patients' deaths. One might think that knowing what to do would come naturally. It doesn't. Almost everyone who has lost a child can tell a horror story about a tactless caregiver.

From the physician's perspective, it isn't always obvious what to do. What do you say on the phone to a mother when her baby has suddenly died? What do you say to a father when you are called suddenly and unexpectedly to the delivery room in the middle of the night and face a baby with an obvious life-threatening malformation? Between figuring out what has happened to the infant, what to do for the infant, and trying to wake up (all in about 30 seconds), it's hard to sound like a competent physician, let alone like an expert psychologist. I have been in both of those situations and other, similar, ones several times; they are not my favorite medical memories.

For a rabbi, it is easier: we are taught the rituals that shape the mourning process and these rituals can make mourning not easier, but as deeply felt as possible so that the tears can fall and the wound can heal. Still, rabbis are just as able to say something tactless as physicians. [JZA, SAA]

When the Child of a Sage Died

It is very useful for physicians, parents, and friends of the bereaved to think about these issues before facing them and to reflect upon the accumulated wisdom of others. The Sages provide us with many examples of how to deal with a child's death. For example, Rabbi Meir and his wife, Bruriah, are said to have lost both their children at once.

Another interpretation: "What a rare find is a capable wife" (Proverbs 31:10). A tale is told of Rabbi Meir that while he was sitting and expounding in the academy on a Sabbath afternoon his two sons died. What did their mother do? She left them both lying on their couch and spread a sheet over them.

At the close of the Sabbath, Rabbi Meir came home from the academy and asked her, "Where are my two sons?"

She replied, "They went to the academy."

He said, "I looked for them at the academy but did not see them."

She [silently] handed him the cup [of wine] for the *Havdalah* benediction, and he pronounced it. Then he asked her again, "Where are my two sons?"

She replied, "Sometimes they go someplace [first]; they will be back presently." She served him [his meal] and he ate. After he recited the Grace after meals she said to him, "Master, I have a question to ask you."

He replied, "Ask your question."

She said, "Master, some time ago a certain man came by and left something on deposit with me. Now he has come to reclaim this deposit. Shall I return it to him or not?"

He replied, "My daughter, is not one who holds a deposit obligated to return it to its owner?"

She said, "Without your opinion [on the matter] I would not give it back to him."

What did she do [then]? She took him by the hand, led him up to the children's room, brought him to the bed, and removed the sheet, so that Rabbi Meir saw them both lying on the bed dead. He burst into tears, saying, "My sons, my sons! My masters, my masters! My natural born sons, and my masters who enlightened me with their [learning in] Torah."

At this point Rabbi Meir's wife said to him, "Master, did you not just now tell me that we must return a pledge to its owner?"

To which he replied, "The Lord has given, and the Lord
has taken away; blessed be the name of the Lord" (Job
1:21). R. Hinina said: In this manner she comforted him
and brought him solace, hence it is said, "What a rare find
is a capable wife!" (Proverbs 31:10). (*Midrash Mishlei*,
chap. 31, on Proverbs 31:10)

In this remarkable story, we see how Rabbi Meir's wife
helps him deal with the sudden death of his two sons. To
fully understand the tale, we must realize that the reason
Bruriah does not tell Rabbi Meir about their sons' deaths
right away is that mourning is prohibited on the Sabbath;
clearly, we would not hide something like that today. This
story is meant to demonstrate how important faith in God
was to Rabbi Meir and his wife and her actions should be
regarded in that light, not taken literally. When it is time
to tell him about the children's death, Rabbi Meir's wife
first reminds him through a story that children are gifts
from God, then allows him to see his dead children, and
finally reminds him once more of how precious God's gift
of children is.

Current Thoughts on Rabbi Meir's Story

If we interpret this story in modern terms, we might argue
with Rabbi Meir's wife's lack of straightforwardness. But
this story is meant to teach us and provide comfort for
those who have lost children, not be a literal guide to
mourning. There are several positive lessons to be learned
from this story regarding how to deal with a child's death.
The first is that Rabbi Meir's wife allows him to see his
children and express his anguish at their death. This is in

keeping with our modern practice of strongly encouraging families to spend time with a newborn (or older child) who has died. Even if it is difficult for the parents at that moment, it is an important part of the grieving process. Another positive aspect to this story is that this couple has shown the strength of their relationship in a moment of great crisis. We note that Rabbi Meir's wife is portrayed as the strong one, even though she has just lost her two sons. There is no hint in this story that the mother cannot deal with her children's death or should be shielded from it.

Occasionally we will hear a father (or a caregiver) say that a newborn's mother shouldn't be told about her infant's death because she cannot deal with it. Early in my training, one of the neonatologists I worked with suggested to me that what the father is probably really conveying is that he is uncomfortable dealing with the mother's expressions of sorrow. [SAA]

What Do You Say When a Child Dies?

There is scarcely anything more difficult than speaking with a family who has lost a child. The things we might say to comfort someone whose elderly parents have died, for example, "He had a good life" or "She was a woman of many accomplishments," do not seem appropriate. Sometimes our attempts to comfort the bereaved parents come too soon and are not successful or appreciated. In the following passage, the Sages recognize how difficult this situation is.

Rabbi Shimon ben Eleazar says: Do not appease your
fellow in the time of his anger; do not console him while
his dead lies before him; do not question him about his
vow at the time he makes it; and do not attempt to see
him at the time of his disgrace. (*M. Pirkei Avot* 4:23)

This passage contains several important ideas about
dealing with human relationships. It states that, in the case
of grief, you should not say things that people cannot hear.
When their dead lie before them, people are filled with
intense grief. At such a moment, before the burial has
taken place, they are frequently unable to hear words of
comfort. They are just hurting too much. Only after the
dead are buried can they accept comfort.

> *This passage also reminds us that if one is unsure of
> what to say, one should say nothing. This is unques-
> tionably true. Almost any consoling statement that
> gives a message more than "I'm terribly sorry" or "My
> thoughts are with you" can be misconstrued or seem
> hurtful and should be carefully thought out first. For
> example, imagine a situation in which a family has
> just had twins or triplets and one of the infants dies.
> We might think that the family shouldn't be too upset
> and should be thankful for the surviving child or chil-
> dren. But to make a comment such as "At least you
> still have one (or two)" ignores the grief this family
> feels at the death of their child. [SAA, JZA]*

In the following passage, we see what happens when a
well-meaning visitor tries to console a grieving father.

A son of one of the notables of Sepphoris happened to
die. . . . R. Yose b. R. Halafta went up to visit him [the

father of the dead boy]. He [the father], seeing him [R. Yose b. Halafta] sitting and laughing, inquired, "Why are you laughing?" He said to him [the father], "We trust in the God of heaven that you will see his [the dead son's] face in the future world." He [the mourner] said to him, "Have I not enough trouble that you have come to trouble me more!" (*Genesis Rabbah* 14:7)

R. Yose b. R. Halafta uses laughter to tell a man that he shouldn't be upset about his son's death because he will be reunited with him in the World to Come. The man is upset by R. Yose's comments and informs R. Yose that his laughter and suggestion are not appreciated. This passage reminds us that not everyone has the same religious perspective and wishes to hear statements such as "Now you have a little angel in heaven" or "It was God's will." Clergy may say these things to families they know well and it will be very comforting. In many situations, however, comments like this are deemed quite inconsiderate.

One of the most frequent questions people have about visiting friends or relatives who have suffered any loss, let alone one as tragic as the death of a child, is "What do I say?" The role of friends is principally to listen, not to speak. Nothing you can say will make it stop hurting. Assurances that everything is all right probably sound false to the person offering them and certainly will grate on the nerves of the mourner. Therefore, the best thing to do is listen and let your family and friends know you are comfortable with their feelings and that those feelings, whatever they may be, are alright. [JZA, SAA]

Miscarriage and Stillbirth

In the ancient world, infant mortality was extremely high, as we have already noted. Perhaps it is for this reason that mourning rituals were not practiced for children who lived less than thirty days.

> Any infant up to thirty days old is carried out in arms (literally "in the bosom") and buried. . . . And they [the people] do not stand in line [to offer condolence to the mourners] on the infant's account, nor do they [need] to recite the [usual] mourner's benediction, nor tender the [usual] condolence to the mourners. (B. Moed Katan 24 a–b)

There are a number of reasons why this teaching, which unfortunately is sometimes still practiced today, needs to be reconsidered. The first is that the infant mortality rate is much lower now than it was in ancient days. The frequency of death in the first month of life in that era meant that it was likely that sitting shivah (the first 7 days of mourning) for every stillborn child, or every child who died in the first month of life, was deemed inappropriate because the community would be in an almost constant state of mourning. It could also have represented a financial hardship, since work is not performed during this first week of mourning.

A second reason for considering changing these mourning practices is that we increasingly recognize the depression and anxiety associated with miscarriages, stillbirths, and infant deaths. In recent years, psychologists have studied grieving reactions associated with such losses. It may well be that the Sages were unaware of the degree to which their wives were affected by such events. A wealth of material in the recent medical literature attests to the tremendous feelings of loss parents experience when an infant dies.

A third reason for reassessing mourning practices is the way in which modern technology has changed the way we relate to our unborn and newborn infants. Sonograms and diagnostic procedures such as amniocentesis allow parents to see and learn about their infants prior to their births. Frequently the parents know the gender of their unborn child. Many parents have had to carefully consider the results of prenatal diagnostic tests. In most cases, the abnormal test result does not presage the finding of a defect, but the level of anxiety and soul searching regarding what this baby means to one's life is intense.

Infant Death

Parents are very aware of the high rate of survival for premature infants. Over the past few years over four-fifths of the very small (1.5- to 2-pound) babies who are inborn (i.e., born at an adjacent hospital's delivery room) at Texas Children's Hospital have survived. Similar results are obtained in many neonatal intensive care nurseries throughout this nation. It may be difficult for parents to accept the death of their sick child knowing that other children (such as the babies in the incubators next to their child's) survived.

Take, for example, the situation of a couple whose child was born 14 weeks early (26 weeks gestation) and weighed nearly 2 pounds at birth. Despite the use of ventilators to help with breathing, medications, and specialized methods of intravenous nutrition, some of these infants do not survive. Yet during the first 30 days, the parents will have had the opportunity to intimately bond with their child. The baby will have been named (neonatal nurses and doctors try to refer to even the smallest babies by their first names). They will have been encouraged to visit, touch, and call in about her frequently. They will undoubtedly have received calls during the day and night about their child and told of problems, tests needed, or even emergency procedures and surgery performed. All for a 2-pound infant! The mother may have provided breast milk for her baby, spending several hours each day using an electric pump (an inglorious procedure), then watched her milk being given to her baby through a feeding tube.

Eventually, after watching a deterioration in their infant's condition, the parents may be asked to allow the physicians to not extend the child's life support if she is without hope of survival. They may even be asked to sign papers to this effect. Many parents hold their infants in their last moments.

Parents experience great grief after the death of their neonate (and after miscarriages and stillbirths as well). In one study, every mother who had experienced such a loss reported definite sadness and preoccupation with thoughts of the dead baby. An article by Emanuel Lewis made the following suggestions regarding helping families deal with stillborn infants. In addition to holding their baby and helping lay her out he suggests:

> Parents should also be persuaded to take an active part in the certification of stillbirth, to name the baby, and to make the funeral memorable. The practice of burial in a

common and nameless grave should be avoided. The family should be encouraged to attend the funeral. . . . It is my impression that if a stillbirth has been a real experience for the family in the ways I have described, mourning will have been facilitated. This leads to fewer psychological problems for the mother and her family.[1]

Miscarriage, stillbirth, and neonatal death are often minimized by others' silence. We hope that the Jewish tradition will not be part of this conspiracy of silence and that infants who live less than thirty days will be mourned fully.

It is important to remember the effects of a neonatal death on the siblings of the child who dies. There are special books available to help parents of young children deal with this situation and, at times, counseling for the siblings may be necessary. I remember one 4-year-old boy who came in to say "Good-bye, I love you" to his (1 pound) brothers right before they died. [SAA]

Ceasing Care

Our tradition stresses the importance of our being created in God's image. To this end, the Sages mandated that an ill or dying person is due the respect each individual receives, even unto the moment of death.

A dying person is regarded as a living entity in respect of all matters in the world. (*B. Semachot* 1:1)

So a person who is only an hour away from death may write a valid will, contract a valid marriage, or execute a valid divorce.

The process of death is likened by the Sages to the flickering of a candle. The dying person may revive intermittently during the process, but the tendency toward death is inexorable.

> Our rabbis taught: One who closes [the eyes of a dying man] at the point of death is a murderer. This may be compared to a lamp that is going out. If a man places his finger upon it, it is immediately extinguished. (B. Shabbat 151b)

The Sages wanted the process of death to take its natural course. We are not to hasten the moment of death, but we are not to delay it unnecessarily, either. As Kohelet remarked, "There is a time to be born and a time to die" (Ecclesiastes 3:2). And when that time has come, we must allow death to approach. Of course, in the case of a child, this may be harder than for any other death. Yet we should not feel guilt at the relief that comes when someone we love who is suffering is finally spared that pain by death. Indeed, we have an example of one who prays for the death of someone she loves who is suffering.

> On the day Rabbi [Yehudah HaNasi] died the rabbis decreed a public fast and offered prayers for heavenly mercy. . . . Rabbi's handmaid ascended the roof and prayed: "The angels want Rabbi [to join them] and the people want Rabbi [to stay with them]. May it be the will of God that the people may overpower the angels." However, when she saw how often he resorted to the privy, painfully taking off his *tefillin* and putting them on again, she prayed, "May it be the will of the Almighty that the angels may overpower the people." As the rabbis incessantly continued their prayers for heavenly mercy she

took up a jar and threw it down from the roof to the ground. For a moment they stopped praying, and the soul of Rabbi departed to its eternal rest. (*B. Ketubot* 104a)

Rabbi was clearly suffering as his death approached, but originally his handmaid prayed that he might continue to live. However, when she saw how painful life was for him, she prayed that he might die. (The Sages wore *tefillin* all day long in those days, but could not wear them in a privy. Therefore, each time Rabbi had to go to the bathroom, he would have to laboriously take them from his head and arm, then put them back on after he came out.) However, the power of all the Sages' prayers kept Rabbi from dying, as if the Sages and the angels were equally matched in a tug-of-war over Rabbi's fate. The handmaid, understanding this, contrived to interrupt the Sages' prayers for a moment, and in that moment, Rabbi was able to die and find relief from his suffering.

This story has obvious implications with regard to an extremely important issue in medicine today. It may be interpreted as indicating that when the situation is hopeless we can stop unnecessary and unproductive efforts to continue life, even though we cannot actively do anything to hasten death. There are few medical questions more in the public mind (except, perhaps, the high cost of medical care) than "When is it time to cease medical care?" There are political movements based on support or opposition to euthanasia and laws and rules have been passed and promulgated regarding this issue as related to newborns.

Modern Jewish medical ethicists have written extensively on this issue. Most of these writers have focused on *halakhah*: what is permissible based on a given Jewish movement's perspective of Jewish law. These issues are bitterly divisive within the medical community as well. Articles and discussions are frequently found in the medical literature regarding when to stop care. This is an issue faced daily by those physicians who frequently care for very sick patients (e.g., intensive care specialists, oncologists, neonatologists, and the like). Obviously, any decision of this nature requires consultation with one's physicians and rabbi, who are familiar with the specifics of the case.

> *When it is finally decided to cease care, the family may feel a sense of relief and then guilt over having felt the relief. The relief is natural and there's no need to feel guilty about it. When a long and futile struggle for life that simply causes everyone pain is over, what else should we feel but relief? Of course, we also feel sadness and resignation, but knowing that someone we love is out of their pain should give us some comfort.* [SAA, JZA]

A Neonatologist's Viewpoint

There is no set answer to the question "When do we cease to care for a baby?" Every situation is unique and we must consider numerous aspects, including the civil laws, when dealing with each case. Some hospitals have ethics committees to help families and medical staff deal with these issues.

> *As a neonatologist, there are two points I'd like to discuss regarding these debates. The first concerns the differences between newborn babies and adults. De-*

tailed criteria have been established for determining brain death in adults based on the absence of signs of life or brain-wave activity. These criteria are critical for allowing cessation of treatment legally, thereby allowing the lifesaving act of organ donation. The halakhic perspective on these criteria may be mixed, but they are widely used and important as the number and types of transplantations increase. In some cases, state laws mandate that the families of a dying person be informed of the options regarding organ donation. Unfortunately, these "brain death" criteria cannot readily be applied to newborns, as the normal pattern of brain-wave activity is very different in newborn babies as compared to older children or adults.[2]

Although doctors and families may perceive a situation as hopeless, it is difficult to apply the legal criteria used in adults to babies, and decisions therefore become more difficult. This has led to widely publicized cases regarding the appropriateness of transplantation in circumstances such as infants born with absence of the brain (anencephaly). In that situation, the child has no chance of living, and the parents may wish to donate the child's organs. But because the baby cannot meet the "brain death" criteria, these transplantations may not be possible without further legal intervention.

The second important point is that it is extremely difficult to make rational ethical decisions in the delivery room. We never know exactly how large a premature baby will be until it is delivered and weighed. And regardless of the size of the baby or nature of her problems, no one can make a completely accurate spot assessment of the future chance of survival or of normal development in the first minute of life. Therefore, the tendency is generally to start treatment if *there is any chance of survival. These situations have led to concerns that neonatal intensive care is creating too many severely handicapped babies by overuse of technology. Further, the cost of such care is staggering. As many articles and discussions in the literature show, neonatologists are not unaware of the problem. But, given the high survival of small premature infants, strict rules regarding who should be treated and how long treatment should be attempted cannot be made as absolute prescriptions.*

I have spent hours discussing options with families prior to the births of their extremely premature or potentially malformed infants. I believe that, increasingly, physicians and ethicists respect the sensitivities and different ideas of infants' families. Civil law, however, has a great deal to say about medical decisions, and decisions regarding limitation of care must follow legal guidelines as well as a family's private preferences. Our society has extremely ambivalent feelings about disabled children and they surface as families deal with the possible consequences of raising a potentially disabled child. [SAA]

Coping with Grief

After the machines have been shut down and the last medications administered, parents must provide for the proper burial of their children.

> A child who lived only one day counts to his father and mother as a fully grown man [in terms of burial]. (*B. Semachot* 3:1)

The passage goes on to describe the minimum burial requirements for children who lived less than thirty days, twelve months, three years, and so forth. There is no debate, however, that the child needs a proper burial. Requirements for burial and mourning rituals are here differentiated. Every infant receives a burial. The ruling regarding children who live less than thirty days refers to sitting *shivah*, observing *sheloshim* (the 30-day mourning period after the burial) and so forth.

Jewish customs regarding mourning are not only ritually significant, they are emotionally important as well. For 7 days after the burial (except on *Shabbat*) the mourners receive visitors in their home and say *Kaddish* (a praise of God recited by mourners) at services held in their home. During this period, food is brought to the mourners and they are kept company. They are encouraged to cry, to grieve, to express the depth of their hurt.

> As a rabbi, I am often worried when people keep a "stiff upper lip" at funerals and during this week of mourning, or when people look too well put together at funerals of close relatives. When someone close to you dies, it's as if someone hands you a bucket of tears and you've either got to cry them away or end up dragging this weight around with you. The healthy thing to do, of course, is what our tradition urges us to do: cry them out immediately so that we don't carry this grief with us in such a painful, weighty way. [JZA]

After this period, we may return to work, but we continue to say *Kaddish* at services in the synagogue for 30 days after the burial (*sheloshim*, which simply means "30"). During this time, we refrain from buying new clothes, going to parties, having haircuts, and the like. This is simply a ritual affirmation of the way we feel anyway. Generally, we don't *want* to go to parties when we still feel so torn up on the inside. If an unexpected invitation comes

our way at this point, we can simply decline it by referring to these rules of mourning. After this, we recite
prayers at *Yizkor* (memorial) services on Yom Kippur, the
last days of Sukkot, Pesach, and Shavuot, and on the
yearly anniversary of the death. Likewise, it is appropriate to give to charity in memory of the child on these
occasions.

And what are we to do with our grief and, perhaps, our
anger? Our relationship with God, like any good relationship, is one in which we are permitted to express all our
feelings and thoughts: love, anger, gratitude, bitterness,
doubt, and faith. Even the angels are allowed to protest
against death. For example, when Rabbi Akiba died a
painful death, martyred by the Romans, the angels cried
out in disbelief and sorrow before God.

> The ministering angels said before the Holy One, blessed
> be He, "Is this Torah, and is this its reward?" [He should
> have been] "from them that die by Your hand, O Lord"
> (Psalm 17:14). He replied to them, "Their portion is in life"
> (Psalm 17:14). (*B. Berachot* 61b)

The angels and God exchange phrases of Psalm 17, verse
14. The angels say that the first phrase of this verse should
refer to Rabbi Akiba who should have died at God's hand
(i.e., a gentle death, not a martyr's death at the hand of
the Romans). God then replies that Rabbi Akiba's portion
is in life, that is, the life of the World to Come.

The angels, and by extrapolation, we, are permitted to
protest what seems an unjust death. We can bring this
injustice to God's attention and demand an explanation.
To a large extent, the explanation that God gives us will
be satisfactory to the degree to which we believe in life

after death. If we believe that there is a life after death, then we will be comforted in the knowledge that our children are receiving a reward in that life. If we do not believe in a life after death, we may still be comforted by the memories we maintain of the time we had together with our children.

After the rituals of mourning have been completed, we may come to a point at which we accept what has happened and be able to live again, even if our lives are changed forever, as did the Sage in the following story:

> R. Abbahu was bereaved. One of his children had passed away from him. R. Jonah and R. Yose went up [to comfort him]. When they called on him, out of reverence for him, they did not express to him a word of Torah. He said to them, "May the rabbis express a word of Torah." They said to him, "Let our master teach us." He said to them, "Now if in regard to the government below, in which there is no reliability, [but only] lying, deceit, favoritism and bribe-taking, which is here today and gone tomorrow, [if concerning that government] it is said, 'And the relatives [of the felon] come and inquire after the welfare of the judges and of the witnesses, as if to say "We have nothing in our hearts [against you], for you judged honestly" (M. Sanhedrin 6:6)' in regard to the government above, in which there is reliability, but no lying, deceit, favoritism, or bribe-taking, and which endures forever and to all eternity, all the more so are we obligated to accept upon ourselves the just decree [of the heavenly government]." (Y. Sanhedrin 6:12, 23d–24a)

This passage uses the Mishnah's ruling that the relatives of an executed felon must eventually give evidence that they have come to terms with the verdict and punishment of their relative. After an appropriate amount of time has passed, the relatives greet the judges and witnesses, conveying that they do not bear a grudge and have accepted what has happened. R. Abbahu compares this procedure of grieving and eventual acceptance to what happens when a child dies, indicating that one must eventually come to terms with such a death in order to be able to go on with one's life.

R. Abbahu's friends are exceptionally tactful. They allow *him* to make this statement of faith rather than trying to convince him of its truth, even though he invites them to try. They allow him to come to his own state of acceptance and to express it in his own way.

The bonds of love are not dissolved upon the death of any family member or loved one. The deceased continue to live in our memories and influence our lives. We can make their memories blessings by letting them influence us to do acts of kindness and righteousness, and in this way bring to our souls some measure of peace. [JZA, SAA]

Notes

Chapter 2: The History of Pediatrics
and Rabbinic Medicine

1. Philippe Aries and Georges Duby, eds., *A History of Private Life* (Cambridge: Belknap Press, 1987), 9.

2. F. H. Garrison, "The History of Pediatrics," in *Abt-Garrison's History of Pediatrics*, ed. Isaac Abt (Philadelphia: W. B. Saunders, 1965) 150.

3. G. B. Avery, ed., *Neonatology–Pathophysiology and Management of the Newborn* (Philadelphia: Lippincott, 1987), 16–18.

4. J. Spago, *The Bitter Cry of the Children* (New York: Macmillan, 1906), 25–26.

5. Garrison. "The History of Pediatrics," 152.

6. Harry Friedenwald, *The Jews and Medicine*, vol. 1 (New York: Ktav, 1967), 17.

7. George F. Still, *The History of Paediatrics* (London: Dawsons, 1965), 8.

8. P. M. Schantz, et al., "Neurocystircercosis in an Orthodox Jewish Community in New York City," *New England Journal of Medicine* 327 (1992): 692–695.

9. Adin Steinsaltz, *Talmud Bavli: Tractate Kiddushin* (Jerusalem: Israel Institute for Talmudic Publications, 1989), 343.

10. Julius Preuss, *Biblical and Talmudic Medicine*, trans. Fred Rosner (New York: Hebrew Publishing, 1983).

Chapter 4: Conception and Pregnancy

1. Thomas Laqueur, *Making Sex: Body and Gender from the Greeks to Freud* (Cambridge: Harvard University Press, 1990), 82.

2. Faith D. Gilroy and Roberta Steinbacher, "Sex Selection Technology Utilization: Further Implications for Sex Ratio Imbalance," *Social Biology* 38:3–4 (1991): 285–288.

3. R. Barkai, "A Medieval Hebrew Treatise on Obstetrics," *Medical History* 33 (1988): 96–119.

4. J. L. Morse, *Clinical Pediatrics* (Philadelphia: Saunders, 1926), 210.

5. Barkai, "Medieval Hebrew Treatise," 96–119.

Chapter 6: Infant Nutrition

1. Thomas Laqueur, *Making Sex: Body and Gender from the Greeks to Freud* (Cambridge: Harvard University Press, 1990), 104–105.

2. Ruth Lawrence, *Breastfeeding: A Guide for the Medical Profession* (St. Louis: Mosby, 1989), 1–27.

3. Faruque Ahmed et al., "Community-Based Evaluation of the Effect of Breast-Feeding on the Risk of Microbiologically

Confirmed or Clinically Presumptive Shigellosis in Bangladeshi Children," *Pediatrics* 90 (1992): 406–411.

4. A. Lucas et al., "Breast Milk and Subsequent Intelligence Quotient in Children Born Preterm," *Lancet* 339 (1992): 261–264.

5. Lawrence, *Breastfeeding*, 220–244.

6. Ibid., 307–309.

7. G. L. Freed et al., "Attitudes of Expectant Fathers Regarding Breastfeeding," *Pediatrics* 90 (1992): 224–227.

8. Lawrence, *Breastfeeding*, 450–464.

9. A. E. Rosner et al., "Birth Interval among Breast-Feeding Women Not Using Contraceptives," *Pediatrics* 86 (1990): 747–753.

10. Adin Steinsaltz, *Talmud Bavli: Ketubot* (Jerusalem: Israel Institute for Talmudic Publications, 1988), 60a, p. 256.

11. Bettye M. Caldwell, "Impact of Day Care on the Child," *Pediatrics* 91 (1993): 225–228.

Chapter 7:
Developmental Stages of Childhood

1. Rachel Anne Rabinowicz, ed., *Passover Haggadah: The Feast of Freedom*, 2nd ed. (New York: The Rabbinical Assembly, 1982), 39.

2. "Use of Infant Walkers," *American Journal of Diseases of Childhood* 145 (1991): 933–934.

3. American Academy of Pediatrics, Committee on Accident and Poison Prevention, "Skateboard Injuries," *Pediatrics* 83 (1989): 1070–1071.

4. P. Benmeir et al., "'Sabbath' Electric Plate Burns: A Ritual Hazard," *Burns* 15 (1989): 39–41.

5. Samuel S. Wineburg, "Factors Affecting Philanthropic Behavior of Jewish Adolescents," *Journal of Social Psychology* 131:3 (1991): 345–354.

Chapter 8:
Parent–Child Relationships: Then and Now

1. Betsy Lozoff et al., "The Mother–Newborn Relationship: Limits of Adaptability," *Journal of Pediatrics* 91 (1977): 1–12.

2. M. Richards, "Bonding Babies," *Archives of Disease in Childhood* 60 (1985): 293–294.

3. Miriam Levi, *Effective Jewish Parenting* (Jerusalem: Feldheim, 1986), 94–95.

4. M. A. Wessel, "The Pediatrician and Corporal Punishment," *Pediatrics* 66 (1980): 639–640.

Chapter 9: Adolescence
and Jewish Parenting

1. Sylvia Barack Fishman and Alice Goldstein, "When They Are Grown They Will Not Depart: Education and the Jewish Behavior of American Adults," *CMJJ Research Report* 8 (March 1993).

2. Tomas J. Silber, "Abortion: A Jewish View," *Journal of Religion and Health* 19:3 (Fall 1980): 238.

Chapter 10: When a Child Dies

1. Emanuel Lewis, "Mourning by the Family after a Stillbirth or Neonatal Death," *Archives of Disease in Childhood* 54 (1979): 304.

2. J. Volpe, "Brain Death Determination in the Newborn," *Pediatrics* 80 (1987): 293–297.

Bibliography

The works listed here were either quoted directly or consulted during the preparation of this book.

Abraham, Abraham S. *The Comprehensive Guide to Medical Halachah.* New York: Feldheim, 1990.

Abrams, Steven, et al. "Mineral Balance and Bone Turnover in Adolescents with Anorexia Nervosa." *Journal of Pediatrics* 123 (1993): 326–331.

Abt, Isaac, ed. *Abt-Garrison's History of Pediatrics.* Philadelphia: Lippincott, 1987.

Ahmed, F., et al. "Community Based Evaluation of the Effect of Breast-Feeding on the Risk of Microbiologically Confirmed or Clinically Presumptive Shigellosis in Bangladeshi Children." *Pediatrics* 90 (1991): 406–411.

American Academy of Pediatrics, Committee on Accident and Poison Prevention. "Skateboard Injuries." *Pediatrics* 83 (1989): 1070–1071.

American Academy of Pediatrics, Task Force on Circumcision. "Report of the Task Force on Circumcision." *Pediatrics* 84 (1989): 388–391.

American Medical Association, Board of Trustees. "Use of Infant Walkers." *American Journal of Diseases of Childhood* 145 (1991): 933–934.

Aries, Phillipe, and Duby, Georges, eds. *A History of Private Life from Pagan Rome to Byzantium*. Cambridge: Belknap Press, 1987.

Avery, G. B., ed. *Neonatology—Pathophysiology and Management of the Newborn*. Philadelphia: Lippincott, 1987.

Barkai, R. "A Medieval Hebrew Treatise on Obstetrics." *Medical History* 33 (1988): 96–119.

Bauchner, H., et al. "Studies of Breast-Feeding and Infection: How Good Is the Evidence?" *Journal of the American Medical Association* 256 (1986): 887–892.

Benmeir, P., et al. "'Sabbath' Electric Plate Burns: A Ritual Hazard." *Burns* 15 (1989): 39–41.

Bialik, Hayim N., et al. *The Book of Legends: Sefer Ha-Aggadah*. New York: Schocken, 1992.

Blackman, Philip. *Mishnayoth*. Gateshead: Judaica Press, 1977.

Brown, Peter. *The Body and Society: Men, Women and Sexual Renunciation in Early Christianity*. New York: Columbia University Press, 1988.

Butte, N., et al. "Human Milk Intake and Growth in Exclusively Breast-Fed Infants." *Journal of Pediatrics* 104 (1984): 187–195.

Caldwell, B. M. "Impact of Day Care on Children." *Pediatrics* 91 (1993): 225–228.

Carey, W. B., et al. "Adolescent Age and Obstetric Risk." In *Premature Adolescent Pregnancy and Parenthood*, ed. E. R. McAnarney (pp. 109–117). New York: Grune and Stratton, 1987.

Cohen, R. "The Life Cycle of the Jewish Family in Eighteenth Century America." In *Papers in Jewish Demography: Proceedings of the Demographic Sessions—7th World Congress of Jewish Studies, Jerusalem, 1977*, ed. U. O.

Schmels et al. Jerusalem: Institute of Contemporary Jewry, Hebrew University, 1980.

DeCasper, A. J., and Fifer, W. P. "Of Human Bonding: Newborns Prefer Their Mothers' Voices." *Science* 208 (1980): 1174–1176.

DeCaspar, A. J., and Spence, M. J. "Prenatal Maternal Speech Influences Newborns' Perception of Speech Sound." *Infant Behavior and Development* 9 (1986): 133–150.

Desmond, M. "A Review of Newborn Medicine in America: European Past and Guiding Ideology." *American Journal of Perinatology* 8 (1991): 308–322.

Diamant, Anita. *The Jewish Baby Book*. New York: Summit Books, 1988.

Eibl, M. M., et al. "Prevention of Necrotizing Enterocolitis in Low-Birth-Weight Infants by IgA-IgG Feeding." *New England Journal of Medicine* 319 (1988): 1–7.

Eilberg-Schwartz, Howard. *The Human Will in Judaism: The Mishnah's Philosophy of Intention*. Atlanta: Scholars Press, 1986.

———. *The Savage in Judaism: An Anthropology of Israelite Religion and Ancient Judaism*. Bloomington, IN: Indiana University Press, 1990.

Encyclopedia Judaica. Jerusalem: Keter, 1972.

Epstein, I., ed. *The Babylonian Talmud*. London: Soncino, 1948.

Feldman, David M. *Marital Relations, Birth Control and Abortion in Jewish Law*. New York: Schocken, 1974.

Findlay, P. *The Story of Childbirth*. Garden City, NY: Doubleday, 1933.

Fishman, Sylvia Barack, and Goldstein, Alice. "When They Are Grown They Will Not Depart: Education and the Jewish Behavior of American Adults." *CMJJ Research Report* 8 (March 1993).

Fletcher, J. C. "Ethics in Reproductive Genetics." *Clinical Obstetrics and Gynecology* 35 (December 1992): 763–782.

Freed, G. L., et al. "Attitudes of Expectant Fathers Regarding Breastfeeding." Pediatrics 90 (1992): 224–227.

Freedman, H., and Simon, Maurice, eds. *Midrash Rabbah*. London: Soncino, 1983.

Freeman, J. M., and Ferry, P. C. "New Brain Death Guidelines in Children: Further Confusion." *Pediatrics* 81: 301–304.

Friedenwald, Harry. *The Jews and Medicine: Essays*. New York: Ktav, 1967.

Gabrioni, C., et al. "Mother-to-Child Transmission of Human Immunodeficiency Virus Type 1: Risk of Infection and Correlates of Transmission." *Pediatrics* 90 (1992): 369–374.

Garza, C., et al. "Special Properties of Human Milk." *Clinics in Perinatology* 14 (1987): 11–32.

Gilroy, Faith D., and Steinbacher, Roberta. "Sex Selection Technology Utilization: Further Implications for Sex Ratio Imbalance." *Social Biology* 38:3–4 (1991): 285–288.

Goldfarb, J., and Tibbets, E. *Breastfeeding Handbook*. London: Libbey, 1980.

Greenberg, Moshe. *The Anchor Bible: Ezekiel, 1–20*. New York: Doubleday, 1983.

Halsey, M. G., et al. "The Role of Animals in Nutrition Research." *Nutrition Today* (July 1993): 19–23.

Hepper, P. G. "Foetal Soap Addiction." *Lancet* 1 (1988): 1347–1348.

Kovar, M. G., et al. "Review of the Epidemiological Evidence for an Association between Infant Feeding and Infant Health." *Pediatrics* (1984): 615–638.

Langman, J. *Medical Embryology*, 3rd ed. Baltimore: Williams and Wilkins, 1975.

Laqueur, Thomas. *Making Sex: Body and Gender from the Greeks to Freud*. Cambridge: Harvard University Press, 1990.

Lawrence, Ruth. *Breastfeeding: A Guide for the Medical Profession*. St. Louis: Mosby, 1989.

Lecanuet, J. P., et al. "Decelerative Cardiac Responsiveness to Acoustical Stimulation in the Near Term Fetus." *Quarterly Journal of Experimental Psychology* 44 (1992): 279–303.

Levi, Miriam. *Effective Jewish Parenting.* Jerusalem: Feldheim, 1986.

Lewis, Emanuel. "Mourning by the Family after a Stillbirth or Neonatal Death." *Archives of Disease in Childhood* 54 (1979): 303–306.

Lozoff, Betsy, et al. "The Mother–Newborn Relationship: Limits of Adaptability." *Journal of Pediatrics* 91 (1977): 1–12.

Lucas, A., et al. "Breast Milk and Subsequent Intelligence Quotient in Children Born Preterm." *Lancet* 339 (1992): 261–264.

Morgenstern, Julian. *Rites of Birth, Marriage, Death and Kindred Occasions among the Semites.* Cincinnati: HUC Press, 1966.

Morse, J. L. *Clinical Pediatrics.* Philadelphia: Saunders, 1926.

Neusner, Jacob. *Judaism and Scripture.* Chicago: University of Chicago Press, 1986.

———, ed. *The Talmud of the Land of Israel: A Preliminary Translation and Explanation.* Chicago: University of Chicago Press, 1984.

Neusner, Jacob, and Sarason, Richard S., eds. *The Tosefta.* Hoboken, NJ: Ktav, 1986.

Oski, Frank. "Iron Deficiency in Infancy and Childhood." *New England Journal of Medicine* 329 (1993): 190–193.

Prema, K., et al. "Lactation and Fertility." *American Journal of Clinical Nutrition* 32 (1979): 1298–1303.

Preuss, Julius. *Biblical and Talmudic Medicine.* Trans. Fred Rosner. New York: Hebrew Publishing Co., 1983.

Rabinowicz, Rachel Anne, ed. *Passover Haggadah: The Feast of Freedom,* 2nd ed. New York: The Rabbinical Assembly, 1982.

Richards, M. "Bonding Babies." *Archives of Disease in Childhood* 60 (1985): 293–294.

Rosner, A. E., et al. "Birth Interval among Breast-Feeding Women Not Using Contraceptives." *Pediatrics* 86 (1990): 747–753.

Rosner, Fred. *Medicine in the Bible and the Talmud*. New York: Ktav, 1977.

Schantz, P. M., et al. "Neurocystircercosis in an Orthodox Jewish Community in New York City." *New England Journal of Medicine* 327 (1992): 692–695.

Silber, Tomas J. "Abortion: A Jewish View." *Journal of Religion and Health* 19 (Fall 1980): 231–239.

Smith, D. W. *Recognizable Patterns of Human Malformation*. Philadelphia: Saunders, 1982.

Soranus. *Gynecology*. Trans. Owsei Temkin. Baltimore: John Hopkins University Press, 1956.

Spago, John. *The Bitter Cry of the Children*. New York: Macmillan, 1906.

Special Task Force. "Guidelines for the Determination of Brain Death in Children." *Pediatrics* 80 (1987): 298–300.

Steinsaltz, Adin. *Talmud Bavli*. Jerusalem: Israel Institute for Talmudic Publications, 1983.

Still, George F. *The History of Paediatrics*. London: Dawsons, 1965.

Stuff, J., and Nichols, B. "Nutrient Intake and Growth Performance of Older Children Fed Human Milk." *Journal of Pediatrics* 115 (1989): 959–968.

Visotzky, Burton L. *The Midrash on Proverbs: Translated from the Hebrew with an Introduction and Annotations*. New Haven, CT: Yale University Press, 1992.

Volpe, J. "Brain Death Determination in the Newborn." *Pediatrics* 80 (1987): 293–297.

Wessel, M. A. "The Pediatrician and Corporal Punishment." *Pediatrics* 66 (1980): 639–640.

Wineburg, Samuel S. "Factors Affecting Philanthropic Behavior of Jewish Adolescents." *Journal of Social Psychology* 131:3 (1991): 345–354.

Zarutskie, P. W., et al. "The Clinical Relevance of Sex Selection Techniques." *Fertility and Sterility* 52 (1989): 891–905.

Index

About the Authors

Judith Z. Abrams serves as rabbi of Congregation Beth El in Missouri City, Texas. She received rabbinic ordination from Hebrew Union College–Jewish Institute of Religion and a Ph.D. in rabbinic literature from the Baltimore Hebrew University. She is the author of *The Talmud for Beginners, Volume I: Prayers* and *The Talmud for Beginners, Volume II: Text,* as well as several prayer books for children. She resides in Texas with her coauthor and husband, Steven, and their three children.

Steven Allen Abrams currently serves as assistant professor of pediatrics at Baylor College of Medicine and as an attending neonatologist at the Texas Children's Hospital and other hospitals in Houston. He received his medical degree from the Ohio State University College of Medicine and serves within Baylor College as a researcher in nutrition at the United States Department of Agriculture/Agricultural Research Service Children's Nutrition Research Center and as a faculty member of the Newborn Section of the Department of Pediatrics. He resides in Texas with his coauthor and wife, Judith, and their three children.